KU-053-159

Yoga made easy

FROM THE NUMBER ONE WOMEN'S HEALTH MAGAZINE

Samantha Magee

in association with

ZeSt
MAGAZINE

COLLINS & BROWN

OLDHAM METRO LIBRARY SERVICE	
A33183417	
Bertrams	23/03/2011
A613 7046M	£9.99
LIM	

8/4/11

This book is to be returned on or before
the last date stamped below.

LIMEHURST LIBRARY

0161 624 0351

LIM

12. MAY 11.

0 3 APR 2013

A3 318 341 7

First published in the United Kingdom in 2011 by
Collins & Brown
10 Southcombe Street
London
W14 0RA

An imprint of Anova Books Company Ltd

Copyright © Collins & Brown 2011

Author: Samantha Magee
Consultant Editor: Heather Thomas at SP Creative Design
Photographer: Caroline Molloy
Model: Funda Onal

Distributed in the United States and Canada by
Sterling Publishing Co, 387 Park Avenue South, New York,
NY 10016-8810, USA

Zest is the registered trademark of The National Magazine
Company Ltd.

All rights reserved. No part of this publication may be
reproduced, stored in a retrieval system, or transmitted
in any form or by any means electronic, mechanical,
photocopying, recording or otherwise, without the
prior written permission of the copyright owner.

ISBN 978-1-84340-527-6

A CIP catalogue for this book is available
from the British Library.

10 9 8 7 6 5 4 3 2 1

Reproduction by Rival Colour Ltd, UK
Printed and bound by 1010 Printing International, China

This book can be ordered direct from
the publisher at www.anovabooks.com

The exercise programmes in the book are intended for people in good
health – if you have a medical condition or are pregnant, or have any
other health concerns, always consult your doctor before starting out.

Contents

Foreword

I'm a huge fan of yoga – I started it myself ten years ago and think it's a fantastic addition to any lifestyle. More than just a ticket to a fabulously toned figure (although it will certainly help you with that!) – yoga will contribute to your overall health and fitness, and can have a hugely positive impact on your state of mind, too.

This book is packed with expert tips and guidance on incorporating yoga into your daily life. Every posture is thoroughly illustrated with step-by-step photography, whether you're just getting started or looking to take your practice up a notch, and accompanied by clear annotations and easy-to-follow instructions. The poses can be simply tailored into a sequence that suits you, or you can choose from the guided workouts at the back of the book. What's more, you'll discover how different postures benefit your body, and learn to practise them accurately, along with meditation and breathing exercises, with the help of expert tips.

But it's not just about the physical side. These days many of us have trouble unwinding or struggle to set aside time just for ourselves. This book is a great solution, with workouts to boost your wellbeing whatever your fitness or flexibility. So, whether you're looking for a quick energy fix, the key to find restful calm before bedtime, or a sure-fire way to tone up all over, you'll find it within these pages.

Good luck and enjoy!

mandie

Mandie Gower
Editor
Zest Magazine

How to use this book

▶▶▶ Yoga is a vast and fascinating subject – it is a science, an exercise system, a philosophy and a way of life. This book aims to give you the confidence to build and develop your own regular yoga practice.

This book outlines many basic, intermediate and advanced yoga postures. We didn't just want to give you the simple stuff, but demonstrate a level of progression to show what can be achieved with focus, commitment and regular practise.

Yoga Made Easy gives you guidelines to practise safely and comfortably in your own home or when you travel. As you learn and practise more, you will begin to incorporate yoga into your whole life.

Each posture or exercise is broken down in a step-by-step format with plenty of pictures and tips to help you develop further. It is important that you read through the information carefully and consciously and then apply the information to the body. Don't rush through the stages! Yoga helps you to develop patience and discipline. As the body is ready to open, you will be able to achieve the more difficult postures with ease and full awareness. So take your time, read the instructions several times and then begin your personal class. Keep going back to the book to check the breathing, alignment and depth in your poses.

The pull-out guide in the back of the book offers a purely visual trigger to all the poses, for you to use as a reference. You can then easily select from them to create a balanced sequence that works for you. To begin with you'll need to follow the written instructions within the book but, once you're familiar with the poses and have memorised the instructions, the pull-out guide should provide an at-a-glance cue.

One of the main benefits of conditioning the body is the direct effect that this will have on your mind. As you practise the postures (asanas), try to keep your mind completely focused on what you are doing. Use the breathing and meditation techniques to develop this

further. A higher level of concentration will allow you to use your breath more efficiently, and to feel where the body might need adjusting or when it feels right to move on a level. You are building breath, body and mind awareness.

The Workouts Made Easy (pages 108–119) have been specifically designed to show you how to incorporate yoga into your lifestyle. The Office Workout gives you handy yoga moves to do discreetly at your desk. These will help you to maintain good posture, strong stomach muscles and keep stress levels low. The 10-Minute Energiser is a quick routine to show you how easy it is to fit yoga into a busy schedule. Even a few minutes of yoga done regularly can provide tremendous benefits! The Tummy Toners, Banish Back Pain and Sleep-well workouts target common problem areas and can be easily done on their own or added on to your regular yoga session.

Remember to stick to the level that feels comfortable for you, where you feel you can breathe freely. Yoga postures should feel challenging, but using your breath correctly should also make them feel slightly effortless. If you are a beginner and a pose feels easy, before you move on to the next level, try to play a little with alignment, depth and breath to see if you can make it more demanding. If it still feels easy, then it's time to move to the next stage.

> Yoga works on breath, conditioning and harmonising the different systems in the body. To achieve advanced postures requires you to master the basics first, allowing the body time to prepare for greater challenges.

THE PROGRAMME AT A GLANCE

Whatever your level, *Yoga Made Easy* provides a 'design your own class' format. When you start your class, make sure you have put aside some personal time, in a quiet place and have your necessary equipment ready, so you can fully focus on your yoga.

Begin with warm-ups; including breathing exercises and Sun Salutations. Then progress through balancing, standing and floor postures, finishing with spinal twists and relaxation. You don't have to do every posture we have shown, but try to create a properly balanced class.

Getting started

Floor postures

Sun salutations

Workouts made easy

Balancing & standing

Relaxation

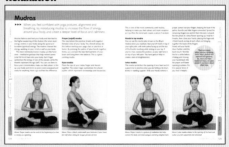

Introduction

There are so many good reasons why you should take up yoga. It's the perfect form of exercise, especially if you have a sedentary lifestyle, sitting in your car or in front of a computer for much of the day. The postures strengthen and loosen your body, building stamina and making your muscles, tendons and ligaments more supple. Your spine and back will be stronger and more flexible, improving your posture and preventing nagging aches and pains. With regular practise, you will feel energised, calmer and more focused and contented – better equipped to deal with day-to-day problems and stressful situations.

What is yoga?

▶▶▶ Yoga is an ancient practice of physical exercises, breathing techniques and internal and external controls that, when practised regularly, creates union of the mind, body and spirit.

INTRODUCTION

GETTING STARTED

BALANCING & STANDING

FLOOR POSTURES

WORKOUTS MADE EASY

RELAXATION

Essentially, yoga means union – of the body, mind and spirit. Its devotees believe that by practising it they will achieve higher body awareness and self-realisation. It is very beneficial, even if you only practise once a week. It calms your mind, makes you feel more energised and full of vitality, balances your physical strength and flexibility, and induces an overall feeling of health and wellbeing. It's also extremely therapeutic, especially if you are recovering from an injury or suffer from nagging aches and pains, particularly in your back.

Body and mind united

Yoga started in India over 5,000 years ago and it's as relevant today as it was in ancient times. The origins of all the modern styles of yoga and the postures we practise now can be found in the fifteenth-century *Pradipika*, a classic manual of Hatha Yoga (see pages 14–15), which described 84 postures (*asanas*). Hatha is just one of the seven major branches of yoga, which can be practised individually or simultaneously.

Hatha Yoga is the most popular form of yoga practised in the Western world. It focuses on bringing awareness to your body by learning and mastering a range of postures, and harnessing your breath (breath control or *pranayama*, as it is sometimes called) to cleanse and balance your body and mind. As your body opens up, it connects more freely with your mind and, ultimately, this leads to spiritual awakening and a more fulfilled, contented and useful life.

Take control

Yoga is a set of practical techniques that we can use to help us find spirituality by uniting our body and mind. It's not a religion or an Eastern philosophy. This misconception about yoga can be off-putting and can make some people reluctant to try it. However, nothing could be further from the truth. Yoga can benefit everyone and, no matter how old or stiff you are, you can still take it up and in a relatively short time you will begin to feel the benefits.

Not only will your body become supple and your muscles more toned but you'll also feel more relaxed and in better control of your life and emotions. If you've never exercised before, have a lot of stress in your life, are overweight, pregnant or disabled, no problem! You can still enjoy all the benefits that practising yoga regularly brings.

Above: Yoga helps us to open up our bodies and minds and embrace the beauty that is around us.

GETTING STARTED

BALANCING & STANDING

FLOOR POSTURES

WORKOUTS MADE EASY

RELAXATION

Branches of yoga

▶▶▶ Hatha Yoga is the most popular branch of yoga in the West, but many other non-physical forms of yoga exist and can be practised in conjunction with Hatha Yoga.

INTRODUCTION

GETTING STARTED

BALANCING & STANDING

FLOOR POSTURES

WORKOUTS MADE EASY

RELAXATION

In ancient times, yoga was sometimes likened to a tree with several branches, each with its own distinctive function, growing out of the main trunk. The major branches correspond to different individual qualities and areas of our lives.

Hatha Yoga – physical

This physical branch of yoga prepares the body for meditation, through a regime of strengthening postures (*asanas*) and cleansing breath control (*pranayama*). Hatha Yoga is sometimes seen as a purification or preparatory state for Raja Yoga (see below). It is the most widely practised and familiar form of yoga.

Bhakti Yoga – devotion

This branch of yoga seeks to encourage selfless love, compassion, fairness and a desire to become one with God. Through developing these qualities in our everyday lives, Bhakti Yoga can help you attain a higher spiritual state. This type of yoga appeals to people with an emotional nature.

Jnana Yoga – wisdom

This yoga of the mind is the most difficult branch of all and requires the integration of all the other branches. Followers believe that an open mind and rational thought are essential for achieving ultimate self-awareness. Not surprisingly, Jnana Yoga appeals to people who are very intellectual. It focuses on the mind and uses a combination of awareness, mind control, study and meditation to free the conscious self and create the True Self.

Karma Yoga – action

This branch of yoga is characterised by selfless work or service, without gain or reward. Karma is both the action and reaction, or cause and effect. The idea is that, by detaching yourself from the gains of your various actions, you learn to release your ego (your conscious self). This type of yoga appeals to positive-thinking people with an outgoing nature who want to make a difference.

Mantra Yoga – sound

Mantra is the yoga of sound. Through using repetitive words and/or syllables (*mantras*), you can focus your mind and become very still and calm. The most familiar form of Mantra Yoga in the West is Transcendental Meditation, as popularised by the Maharishi Yogi and the Beatles. 'Om' is the most commonly used mantra, and helps to connect the body with universal vibrations.

Raja Yoga – meditation

This type of mind control is often called 'royal yoga' because it enables the yogi who practises it to acquire ultimate self control and become Ruler of His/Her Mind. As you will discover later in this book (see pages 122–123), meditation is a useful technique for calming and controlling the mind. When your mind is still, self-realisation becomes clear and possible.

Tantra Yoga – awakening

This branch of yoga teaches us to look for sacred experiences in our lives as well as controlling our sexual energy and uniting the male and female energies in the body. Tantra Yoga focuses on using pleasure, vision and ecstasy through yoga and meditation to heighten body energy and achieve enlightenment.

Styles of yoga

▶ ▶ ▶ There are several different styles of yoga. Each one places emphasis on a different aspect, such as physical exertion, breath control, or opening of the spine and heart.

INTRODUCTION

GETTING STARTED

BALANCING & STANDING

FLOOR POSTURES

WORKOUTS MADE EASY

RELAXATION

Hatha Yoga is the most prevalent form of physical yoga in the West, but there are several other styles, and one of these may suit you better. Over the years, Indian Yogis and Western yoga teachers have developed new systems, adapting the ancient postures and making them more appropriate to the modern world. Some styles focus more on breath work and meditation, while others are more strenuous and physically demanding. This wide range of styles has increased yoga's appeal to people all over the world. No matter how or why you come to yoga, you will soon realise the benefits, and it will become your lifelong companion. Look at the following styles to decide which is the right one for you.

Above: Prayer mudra – a hand position that neutralises the positive and negative sides of the body and creates centring (see pages 124–125).

Hatha Yoga

Hatha means 'force' or 'will', and this style of yoga focuses on gaining control over your body through a combination of physical poses and breathing exercises. Also known as 'yoga for the body', it uses the postures to create an opening in your body, enabling your mind to prepare itself to meditate. A Hatha Yoga class consists of breath work and the slow flow between postures. It is less rigorous than Ashtanga or Bikram Yoga.

Anusara Yoga

This system, which is based on Hatha Yoga and was founded by John Friend in 1997, is becoming increasingly popular. *Anusara* means 'flowing with grace', 'following your heart' and 'going with the flow'. It is very uplifting and heart-oriented, seeking the good in people and celebrating integrity and truthfulness. The postures are expressed from the inside out (see pages 18–19), and are used to create the greatest expression of individual goodness, grace and power.

Ashtanga Yoga

Created by K. Pattabhi Jois at his school in Mysore, India in 1948, Ashtanga, or 'Power', Yoga combines challenging postures with breath work. The postures are performed in a flowing sequence (*vinyasa*), which produces internal heat and external sweating leading to detoxification. This type of yoga focuses on physical strength, stamina and flexibility, and you need to master each sequence before moving onto the next.

Bikram Yoga

This Hatha Yoga system, which incorporates 26 postures and two breathing exercises, was developed by Bikram Choudhury. Also known as 'Hot Yoga', the classes are held in a studio heated to 35–38°C (95–100°F)

INTRODUCTION

GETTING STARTED

BALANCING & STANDING

FLOOR POSTURES

WORKOUTS MADE EASY

RELAXATION

Zest tip

When trying different styles of yoga, be open to the experience, as they each will have different benefits. Also try to find a teacher that inspires you, makes you feel secure and confident and teaches from a basis of safety and compassion.

to promote sweating and stretching, prevent injury, detoxify and realign the body, and boost the immune system. Bikram Yoga works by using the 'tourniquet effect'. Through compressing joints and organs, blood pressure builds up and, when it's released, the compressed area is flooded with oxygenated blood, leading to increased healing. This rigorous form of yoga is not for everyone, but it can be helpful for back and knee problems.

Iyengar Yoga

Developed by B.K.S. Iyengar, this style of yoga focuses on the precise details and alignment of postures. A variety of props, such as blocks, chairs and straps, are used to help you achieve the correct posture. Although it's quite a gentle system, it is challenging because some postures are held for long periods of time.

Kundalini Yoga

Founded by Yogi Bhajan, Kundalini Yoga is based on releasing the spiritual ('serpent power') energy that is stored at the base of the spine. It uses a combination of breath work, chanting and postures to intensify your meditative powers, which ultimately awakens the energy. This yoga system is very gentle, with less emphasis on physical postures.

Jivamukti Yoga

This system of yoga was founded in the 1980s by Sharon Gannon and David Life. It combines vigorous posture work, meditation, chanting and the study of ancient texts to help you achieve a deeper level of yogic understanding.

Sivananda Yoga

Developed by the charismatic Swami Sivananda Saraswati, Sivananda Yoga is based on the Gurukula system – *guru* means 'teacher' and *kula* means 'home'. It incorporates breath control (*pranayama*), classic postures (*asanas*), relaxation, positive thinking, prayer, chanting and meditation. It is usually taught in a structured course, and there are many centres around the world.

Above: Bow pose – an active back bend that helps to energise the central nervous system and keep the spine flexible (see pages 84–85).

Above: Crow pose – an arm balance that strengthens the arms and wrists, focuses the mind and enhances your powers of concentration (see pages 76–77).

Work your body inside out

INTRODUCTION
GETTING STARTED
BALANCING & STANDING
FLOOR POSTURES
WORKOUTS MADE EASY
RELAXATION

▶▶▶ The body is an eco-system, full of energy, made up of individual systems that work by constantly balancing and reacting to each other. Yoga helps to maintain the body's harmony, keeping mind and body connected.

Your body is made up of several different systems, which complement each other and work together. What makes yoga so special, unlike most types of exercise, is that it works holistically on all these systems to create balance and harmony. This is very beneficial, making you feel calmer and more relaxed as well as physically fitter. Many of us discover yoga because we want to heal an injury or deal more effectively with everyday pressures and stress, but yoga also helps to improve our overall health and wellbeing because it works the whole body inside out, benefiting all the different systems.

Skeletal system

Your spine is so important, not only because it houses the spinal cord connecting the rest of your body to your brain, but also because, in yoga, it is the main energy channel. If your spine is well aligned

Above: Rounded forward stretch – a strong spinal stretch that helps to maintain flexibility and space in the spinal column. Also beneficial for the endocrine and nervous systems.

you can increase the flow of *prana* (energy and life force) through your body, stimulating the nerve endings that send instructions and information to your brain. By opening up your spine, you can enhance the vibration and energy throughout your whole body. And, by improving your posture and flexibility, you'll help prevent back pain and develop a full range of motion, slowing down the ageing process, too!

Central nervous system

This is housed in your spine and brain, and controls all your mental and physical activities. The central nervous system is the 'information highway' of the body. Nerve impulses are triggered by sensory information and then distributed throughout the body, resulting in a mental or physical reaction. In yoga, breath is the connection between your mind and body. Through a combination of breathing exercises and physical postures, you can keep this system healthy and functioning well.

Muscular system

Your muscles make it possible for you to move your body as well as your internal organs. Muscles are arranged in overlapping layers in pairs, contracting and relaxing in opposition to each other. If you want strong muscles, you need to exercise them regularly. Performing the yoga postures can stretch them out and provide a wide and balanced range of motion.

Respiratory system

When you breathe in (inhale), air enters your body through your nose or mouth and then passes down your windpipe into your lungs. The muscles between your ribs contract, pulling your ribcage up and out, and your lungs expand as they suck in more air. When you breathe out (exhale), your chest muscles relax, your ribcage sinks and your lungs contract, squeezing out the air. Yoga teaches you to be more aware of your breathing and to breathe in a more regulated way, helping you to perform the postures more easily and to be more in touch with your body and inner self.

Endocrine system
The endocrine system is one of your body's most important systems. The endocrine glands (thyroid, adrenal, pituitary, pancreas and ovaries) produce hormones, which regulate your body. The endocrine system is the 'control panel' of the body. Some yoga postures increase blood supply to these glands, helping to keep them healthy, balanced and running smoothly.

Cardiovascular system
A healthy heart and cardiovascular system are essential for your wellbeing. Yoga can improve your circulation, so more blood and oxygen are distributed through your body and brain – making you more mentally alert, your body more energised, and nourishing your joints, muscles and organs as well.

Digestive system
Your digestive tract extends from your mouth to your bottom. Inside it, the food you eat is digested and processed, and any waste products are expelled from your body. Practising yoga regularly can improve your digestion and help speed up the elimination process.

How the postures work
The yoga postures (*asanas*) are the medium you use to exercise and improve all these different systems. They stretch and open your body, creating space through a combination of slow, rhythmic movements and regulated breathing. All the postures should encompass the following:

★ Breath
★ Alignment/grounding
★ Stretching or expanding
★ Stillness or lightness
★ Balance.

If you follow the yoga philosophy outlined in this book, do the breathing exercises and relaxation techniques, and make time to practise the postures on a regular basis, you will feel fitter, healthier, happier and well chilled out!

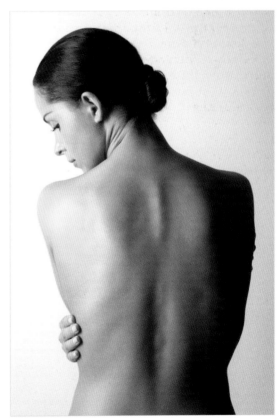

Above: Yoga postures help to create a healthy and strong spine. All other systems in the body will benefit, as they lead off the incredible bodily structure that is the spine.

INTRODUCTION

GETTING STARTED

BALANCING & STANDING

FLOOR POSTURES

WORKOUTS MADE EASY

RELAXATION

Yoga as a lifestyle

▶▶▶ When you first begin yoga, it may simply be an exercise. As your body and mind begin to detox, connect and become stronger, yoga will become a greater part of your life.

INTRODUCTION

GETTING STARTED

BALANCING & STANDING

FLOOR POSTURES

WORKOUTS MADE EASY

RELAXATION

Yoga is more than just a physical exercise – it's a way of life, which addresses our physical, mental and spiritual needs, and provides a framework for our day-to-day lives. This all-embracing philosophy is just as relevant today as when it originated in ancient times.

The eight paths of yoga

When you decide to take up yoga, you are embarking on a journey of self-discovery, which will culminate in achieving mental and physical union. The ancient scripts of the Yoga Sutras outlined a series of steps that you can take to purify your mind and body and live a better life. These paths are listed below.

Yamas: These moral values can bring harmony to our personal relationships and provide a set of ethical guidelines for how we can live – peacefully and with integrity. Traditionally, they encompassed being truthful, never stealing or harming anyone, and not being greedy. We can follow these principles today by being honest, considerate, compassionate, understanding and loving.

Samadhi: This is the final path when we achieve mystical absorption – a state of personal freedom in which the body and mind fully connect to achieve a state of super-consciousness.

Dhyana: From dharana we move on into a state of meditation, where our minds are totally still and emptied of all external thoughts.

Dharana: This path of yoga is when we move on to practising single-minded concentration.

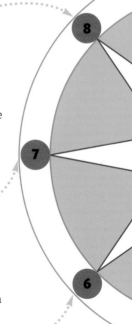

Niyamas: This set of restraints governs how we conduct ourselves and interact with other people. They help us to develop internally and to grow spiritually, so we can enjoy healthy, fulfilled lives. They include purity of mind, contentment, staying calm, self-study and meditation.

Pranayama: Yoga teaches us breathing techniques that help us to absorb *prana*, the life force, opening up our self-awareness and connecting body and mind.

Asanas: These postures (called poses in this book) are the path to greater physical and mental balance and wellbeing.

Pratyahara: As we turn inwards and focus internally, we withdraw from the external world and the sensations of touch, taste, smell and sound, and prepare the mind for stillness.

FIVE PRINCIPLES TO GUIDE OUR LIVES TODAY

Five basic principles can help you achieve a more yogic way of living.

1. **Proper breathing** – *pranayama* (see pages 22–24).

2. **Proper exercise** – *asanas* (see opposite).

3. **A healthy diet that is nourishing, well-balanced and based on natural foods** – helps to keep your immune system strong, your body supple and your mind calm and clear.

4. **Positive thinking and meditation** – help banish negative thoughts and still your mind. This is important for managing stress in your life.

5. **Proper relaxation** – releases mental and physical tension, so your whole body feels rejuvenated, restored and more energetic.

INTRODUCTION

GETTING STARTED

BALANCING & STANDING

FLOOR POSTURES

WORKOUTS MADE EASY

RELAXATION

Breathing

INTRODUCTION

GETTING STARTED

BALANCING & STANDING

FLOOR POSTURES

WORKOUTS MADE EASY

RELAXATION

▶▶▶ Breathing is a natural process, but very rarely do we stop and think about how important it is. Breathing properly increases flow of energy, nourishes and detoxifies the body and, ultimately, is the connection between body and mind.

Breath control is essential in yoga. In fact, breath is life. It's the spark that lights up your body and mind, and it's surprising that most of us pay so little attention to our breathing. We could live for over a month without food, several days without water, but we'd only survive a few minutes without air.

Breath awareness

By becoming aware of the breath within you – which flows, naturally and unrestricted, through your body – you'll learn how to be present in the moment and how to experience the universal life force (*prana*) that exists inside us all. As we get older, we tend to breathe less deeply (more into the top part of our lungs), so we need to retrain our bodies to breathe more fully, making use of our entire respiratory system. On a practical level, in yoga, this means learning to breathe with your mouth closed, inhaling until your lungs are full and then exhaling until they empty. This is really beneficial, for the following reasons:

★ It increases your breath capacity
★ It exercises your abdominal region
★ It massages your heart and internal organs.

Breathing exercises

When you practise yoga, you use special breathing techniques (*pranayama*) to increase your breath capacity – *prana* means 'breath' or 'life force' while *yama* means 'control'. You need to do these breathing exercises to detox your body, cleanse the cells and nerve channels and get ready to control your inner energies. Pranayama breathing exercises are good for both your body and mind.

★ **Your body:** Breath control helps to reduce toxins and bodily waste; aid digestion; increase oxygen levels throughout the body; prevent disease; and de-stress and relax your body.

★ **Your mind:** Deep breathing is very calming and helps you develop good concentration and focus.

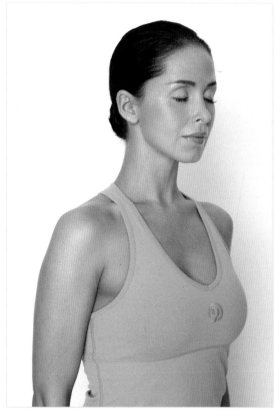

Above: By closing the eyes, more awareness can be focused on breathing through the nose to create a full breath.

As your mind functions more clearly, you can handle your reactions better, avoid arguments, and make decisions more quickly and effectively. And, by boosting your self-control, you also have more control over your body.

Breathing techniques

There are many different breathing techniques, including ujjayi, kapalbhati, bhastrika (bellows breath) and alternate nostril breathing (see pages 38–39), but most of them encompass the following:

★ **Inhalation:** When you breathe in, you bring in energy, which nourishes your body. By breathing through your nose, the *prana* reaches the olfactory organs that stimulate your central nervous system and brain.

★ **Retention:** Holding your breath increases your lung capacity, giving you time and space for the energy to flow through your body and into your mind.

★ **Exhalation:** When you breathe out, waste products and toxins are eliminated from your lungs and body. The more air you expel, the greater your next fresh breath will be, making this a good way to detox. You can also use exhalation as a release breath to help you move through difficult postures.

Active breathing

When you breathe normally you tend to use your whole body: you may lift your shoulders slightly, your tummy may move in and out as you inhale and exhale, and you probably breathe through your mouth. The action is automatic and unconscious. In pranayama breathing, however, your brain is conscious, but most of your body is passive and your lungs and abdomen do all the work. There are three types of breath: shallow (high), intercostal (middle) and abdominal (low). Yogic breathing uses all of these regions for a maximum breath. By expanding your ribcage and lungs to their full

Above: Alternate nostril breathing (see page 37) is a pranayama breathing technique.

capacity, you engage your abdomen and this affects your diaphragm. This is active breathing, as opposed to regular breathing, which is passive.

Linking your body and mind

Breathing is the key to connecting your mind with your body, making it a very important and essential part of yoga. By teaching yourself to breathe deeply, you'll learn how to steady your mind, improve your concentration and nourish your body as well.

Unless you learn how to breathe properly and use the breath to help control your mind, it's very difficult to master the art of meditation. If you've ever tried to just sit down and meditate without any preparation, you'll know what this means. This is why it's usually best to do your relaxation or meditation at the end of a yoga session, when your mind is more still after breathing and posture work.

INTRODUCTION

GETTING STARTED

BALANCING & STANDING

FLOOR POSTURES

WORKOUTS MADE EASY

RELAXATION

INTRODUCTION

GETTING STARTED

BALANCING & STANDING

FLOOR POSTURES

WORKOUTS MADE EASY

RELAXATION

Make sure you always pay attention to your breathing when you're performing the postures (*asanas*). You'll be amazed at how big a difference this makes. You'll be able to hold postures longer, find ease in difficult positions and make faster progress, making your yoga much easier and more satisfying. Remember that everything you do in yoga should be 'breath-led motion' – being aware of your breathing is an integral part of performing the physical postures. As your body gets fitter, stronger, more flexible and supple, your mental skills will be enhanced, too, and your mind will be clearer and more focused. It's a win–win situation!

Zest tip

When you practise a posture and it starts to feel difficult, try to breathe more deeply through the nose. Usually, when you breathe deeper, you will have the energy and focus to maintain the posture for longer and achieve more benefits from the work you are doing!

Below: Lying on your back with the palms of your hands gently on your stomach is a great way of understanding the use of abdominal muscles in active breathing.

Safety first

▶▶▶ It's important to be safety-conscious in your yoga sessions, especially if you are not fully fit, toned and supple. After all, yoga is meant to heal your body, not aggravate any existing injuries or weaknesses.

Get lined up

When you practise postures, do make sure that your body is correctly aligned and that your weight-bearing joints are supported. Your feet are key, as alignment begins from this base. When the feet are correctly set up and aligned, you will feel more balanced and can start building the posture from this foundation.

Don't go for the burn!

Be aware – always listen to your body and take notice of what it's telling you. A feeling of deep stretching is fine, but you should never feel pain. As soon as this happens, back off immediately. You may be pushing yourself too far too soon, in which case you must slow down and progress gradually, one step at a time. The body will open more fully when it is ready to. You might find that a small adjustment or modification to the posture will make it safer and ultimately easier to maintain.

Balance your sessions

To practise yoga safely, you need to put yourself through a whole range of movements, including standing, sitting, lying down, balancing, bending and twisting. This will make you feel more refreshed and energised afterwards. As well as balancing your sessions, you need to balance the postures. You can achieve this by doing counterposes – postures that balance previous ones and stretch your spine or muscles in the opposite direction to return the body to a neutral or harmonious position. So a twist to the right is followed by a twist to the left, and a forward bend is followed by a back bend.

Get ready!

Before you start, you'll need a few basic items of equipment:

★ A good-quality non-slip mat
★ A folded blanket for some of the sitting and floor postures
★ A yoga strap to help you stretch further
★ Yoga blocks – you might find these useful if you are less flexible, as they can provide support.

Always wear comfortable clothes that aren't restrictive and move with your body. Tight bottoms or shorts are best, so you can see your knees, ankles and feet. Tie long hair back off your face and take off your watch, jewellery and make-up.

Practise yoga on an empty stomach. Try not to eat for two to three hours before your session. Drink some water about an hour or two before you start, but try not to drink while you're practising yoga as this can cool the body internally. And, finally, if you keep an open mind and are kind and loving to yourself, your yoga routine will be very rewarding.

INTRODUCTION

GETTING STARTED

BALANCING & STANDING

FLOOR POSTURES

WORKOUTS MADE EASY

RELAXATION

Design your own programme

▶▶▶ Life can be busy and hectic, but making time for a regular yoga session will give you great benefits. Design a class that fits into your life and start to feel the rewards.

INTRODUCTION

GETTING STARTED

BALANCING & STANDING

FLOOR POSTURES

WORKOUTS MADE EASY

RELAXATION

Begin by setting aside a regular slot in your daily routine for your yoga practice – whatever works best for you. It might be early in the morning before you get dressed and leave for work, in the evening when you come home, or just before going to bed when you are feeling more relaxed. Begin with some short sessions of 10–15 minutes and then gradually lengthen these as you become more proficient and can do more strenuous poses.

Some of the yoga exercises may not feel very natural at first, but it won't be too long before your body feels more conditioned, supple and flexible and you can perform them more easily.

In fact, when you start experiencing the benefits that yoga brings and feel fitter and healthier, you'll want to do more. You may even find yourself getting tense if you

have a particularly hectic week and it's difficult to fit in your usual yoga session. Don't worry if this happens; when things quieten down, you'll soon get back into your old routine. Just design your own programme and make it flexible enough to accommodate any changes in the pattern of your life.

Build a personal yoga class
All yoga sessions, whether they're performed on your own at home or by going to a local class, should be balanced and encompass a range of exercises. These include a warm-up, breathing exercises, a variety of postures which include a full range of movements for your spine – forwards, backwards, sideways, counterposes, balances and twists – and a relaxation session at the end. There are lots of poses to learn in this

Zest tip
Don't eat a heavy meal before your yoga session – always eat afterwards. Even if you have just a light meal or snack, you should wait two hours before doing your yoga.

Left: Spinal twists help to equalise and detox the spine, so they are done at the end of a session.

book, but you could start off with a simple programme that includes the following:

★ **Mountain** (see pages 48–49) – a centring and foundation pose
★ **Sun Salutations** (pages 40–41) – to get you loosened up and in the mood
★ **Standing Camel** (see pages 50–51) – a back bend
★ **Wide-leg Forward Bend** (see pages 52–53) or **Forward Stretch** (see pages 86–87) – a forward bend
★ **Triangle** (see pages 58–59) – a side stretch
★ **Tree** (see pages 66–67) – a balancing pose
★ **Simple Seated Twists** (see pages 102–103) – a twist
★ **Corpse** (see pages 106–107) – relaxation.

Get in the mood

If you're at home, find a quiet place where you won't be disturbed or interrupted. Remember, this is your time! You may wish to do the postures in front of a full-length mirror to make sure you are doing them correctly. You may find it helpful to place a soothing object or picture in your field of vision – you can focus on this when you are concentrating or meditating. Wear some supportive clothing – whatever feels comfortable – and organise all the equipment you need before you start: a yoga mat, chair, a strap or blocks if you need them. Unplug the phone or set it to answering machine, turn off your mobile and you're ready to go.

IF YOU'RE PREGNANT...

Being pregnant doesn't mean that you can't exercise. On the contrary, yoga will be tremendously beneficial during pregnancy as it teaches you how to relax, makes you more aware of your breathing, keeps the body strong and supple, stretches out your muscles, and helps you understand the workings of your body. It also opens your hips and strengthens your legs, which are vital during labour. Your posture will improve, too, helping you to feel more comfortable and giving your baby more room to grow and stretch inside you. And, most importantly, you will not only transmit your inner feelings of calm and wellbeing to your baby, but you are also less likely to experience tension, fatigue and insomnia.

CAUTION!
The most critical time in your pregnancy is between weeks 8 and 13, so practise only really gentle exercises and postures during this period. If in doubt, check with your doctor or yoga teacher.

Pregnancy checklist:

★ Do not practise breath retention (see page 23).

★ As your bump gets bigger, adapt and modify the postures to allow sufficient space for it, e.g. legs wider apart or knees bent when you forward bend and no compression postures.

★ Rest frequently in one of the relaxation poses (such as Child's Pose – see page 45) or by lying on your left side to increase blood flow to your baby and yourself.

★ Never push yourself too far, so that you get over-heated or breathless. You should feel like you could carry on a conversation while exercising.

★ Stop immediately if you feel any discomfort or pain.

★ NOTE: *Yoga Made Easy* is not a pregnancy yoga book, although some of the postures are safe to practise while pregant, under the guidelines we have listed above and if you are a regular practitioner. Always check with your yoga teacher or a pregnancy yoga book that you are performing the modified postures correctly.

INTRODUCTION

GETTING STARTED

BALANCING & STANDING

FLOOR POSTURES

WORKOUTS MADE EASY

RELAXATION

Your personal development

INTRODUCTION

GETTING STARTED

BALANCING & STANDING

FLOOR POSTURES

WORKOUTS MADE EASY

RELAXATION

▶▶▶ Yoga is a journey. As you practise regularly, your body and your mind will open, expand and develop. So practise, practise, practise and see where it takes you.

In their most basic form, the yoga postures in this book are an effective and enjoyable way to exercise, but really they are far more important than this. You can transform your yoga sessions, lifting them from simple physical exercise to a more holistic level by the way you breathe and the way you view them emotionally. This will enhance your yoga practice, improve your technique when you perform the postures and aid your personal development.

Develop your technique

When you take up yoga, follow these simple guidelines and principles to give your sessions more structure. You'll not only develop a better technique when you're doing the postures, but you'll also experience greater results on all levels and will feel more satisfied and generally fulfilled as a person.

★ Intention

This is important if you are to achieve one-point focus through uniting your mind and emotions. Although your mind provides direction, it is your emotions that give the direction power. Therefore, always try to approach each session with a personal thought or higher intention, such as balance, stillness, strength or clarity. You will get more out of your yoga if you do this and set yourself specific targets.

★ Breath

Breath-led movement is vital for good yoga practice and technique. Always begin your breathing practice simply by standing or sitting still and inhaling and then exhaling through your nose. When this feels rhythmic or regular, you can start incorporating the physical movements (postures). Remember to breathe whenever you are changing a posture. If your breathing gets lost or less important at any point, just come back to it and then resume the posture. Breathing is the fuel for the physical work you do, and it also boosts the connection between your body and mind.

★ Movement

Aligning your body properly during posture work is very important for getting the most out of your yoga. When the body is aligned, the major bones and joints will be supported and energy will flow more easily. When you practise the poses throughout this book, look at the images and follow the instructions carefully to make sure you have the correct body alignment with your spine, arms, shoulders, hips, legs and feet in the right position.

★ Take it easy

Always perform the postures at a sustainable level, so your breath can flow easily. Don't push yourself too far or too fast – just take it gradually and, in each new session, build on what you achieved in the last one. Try to set up a posture, then achieve a point where you feel a deep stretch, but can still breathe comfortably. There's no need to rush – yoga is all about stillness and calming your mind as well as getting fit. As your body becomes stronger and more supple, you can start taking the postures a little further as well as introducing more advanced ones. You will find suggestions for this throughout the book.

Zest tip

It is good to set goals within everything you do, as this creates focus and determination. But don't become fixated on getting to the ultimate goal or perfect posture. Yoga teaches you that the journey is far more important than reaching the finish line – the finish line is constantly changing and life happens during the journey!

INTRODUCTION

GETTING STARTED

BALANCING & STANDING

FLOOR POSTURES

WORKOUTS MADE EASY

RELAXATION

Getting started

Now that you've decided to take up yoga, it's time to start putting all you've read into practice and learn how to perform the postures. A good way to begin your yoga session is by warming up your body and doing some simple breathing exercises. You can then progress to the Sun salutations – a flowing sequence of postures that work in harmony with each other to stretch out your muscles and strengthen your body. You'll soon be doing these naturally and automatically, without looking at the instructions, as your body and mind master these new challenges, leaving you physically and mentally refreshed and invigorated.

Warm-up

▶▶▶ Always take time out to warm up before you start your yoga session. This warms up your muscles, loosens your joints, focuses your concentration and gets you in the mood.

INTRODUCTION

GETTING STARTED

BALANCING & STANDING

FLOOR POSTURES

WORKOUTS MADE EASY

RELAXATION

BEST FOR MEDITATION

Easy pose

Start with this pose to straighten and stretch out your spine, release any tension in your hips and groin, and help you become calm, still and focused. Beware: the name is deceptive and it may not be as easy to do as it looks if you're a beginner. However, persevere and the more you practise, the more comfortable it'll become.

1 Sit up straight, seated on the floor with your arms at your sides and legs extended in front of you. Bend your knees out to the sides and then cross them, so the top of your right foot is on the floor in front of your lower left leg, and the top of your left foot is on the floor inside your right thigh. Turn the soles of your feet up towards the ceiling.

2 Keeping your buttocks and tops of your feet on the floor, edge your knees in closer together and relax your legs down towards the floor. Rest your palms on your knees, your fingers curling gently round them, and relax your shoulders and arms.

3 Inhale and stretch your spine upwards and pull the abdominal muscles in gently to support the back. Focus on deep and conscious breathing, allowing the breath to move freely in and out of the nose. Try to remain in this position for 1–2 minutes.

4 To increase the spinal stretch, interlace your fingers in front of you, inhale and raise your arms fully overhead as you stretch up. Hold the stretch for a few breaths and exhale, release the fingers and stretch the arms outwards and down. Repeat several times.

5 Release your legs slowly. Gently shake them out and rotate the ankles to return circulation to these areas.

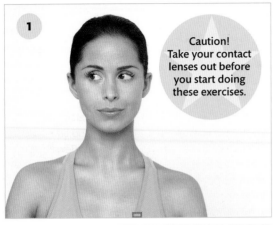

1

Caution!
Take your contact
lenses out before
you start doing
these exercises.

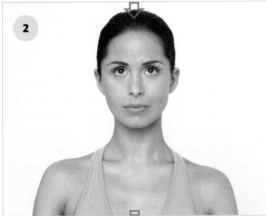

2

5

WARM UP YOUR EYES

This series of exercises will help strengthen your eye muscles and reduce eye strain, keeping your eyes healthy. When you do them, only move your eyes and keep your head perfectly still and centred. Sit in a comfortable position with your back straight, shoulders relaxed, chin parallel to the floor, looking straight ahead – don't move your head!

1 Move your eyes to look to the right as far as you can. Now move them to look to the left as far as you can. Repeat 3 times.

2 Keeping your head perfectly still and level, look up towards the ceiling and then move your gaze down to the floor. Repeat 3 times.

3 Now repeat step 1, looking as far to the left and then to the right as you can.

4 Move your eyes slowly clockwise in a circle 3 times. Then move them anticlockwise 3 times.

5 Extend your left arm out in front of you at eye level, make a fist and point your thumb upwards. Make a fist with the right hand and hold the right thumb upwards, halfway between your eyes and your raised left thumb and focus your gaze on the thumb furthest away from you. Next, focus both eyes on the nearer thumb. Repeat 3 times.

Zest tip

If the knees rest above the hips in Easy Pose, and this is uncomfortable, place a block or blanket underneath the buttocks to raise the hips and drop the knees.

INTRODUCTION

GETTING STARTED

BALANCING & STANDING

FLOOR POSTURES

WORKOUTS MADE EASY

RELAXATION

INTRODUCTION

GETTING STARTED

BALANCING & STANDING

FLOOR POSTURES

WORKOUTS MADE EASY

RELAXATION

WARM UP YOUR WRISTS AND HANDS

Use the following stretches as part of your usual yoga warm-up to loosen up your wrists and hands. If your wrists or hands feel stiff or tight between postures, just repeat these exercises and they'll soon feel more relaxed.

Hand stretch

1 Sit or stand up straight and make a fist with both your hands in front of your chest. Your hands should be facing each other with the wrists and knuckles touching.

2 Inhale and slowly start opening your fingers until your fingertips and palms come together. Stretch out your fingers, thumbs and through your whole hands until they are fully extended and you can really feel a deep stretch across the whole hand.

3 Exhale and fold your fingers back down into a fist again. Repeat several times.

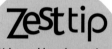

Zest tip

Wrist and hand exercises can be performed at the office, as they help to prevent RSI (repetitive strain injury).

Wrist rolls

1 Stretch out your right arm directly in front of you, parallel to the floor. Make a fist with your hand and rotate your wrist clockwise and then anticlockwise.

2 Repeat several times with the right wrist, then release, swap arms and repeat with the left wrist.

Wrist and hand extensions

1 Sit on the floor with your back straight, legs extended in front of you, or sit in Easy Pose (see page 32). Place your hands under your buttocks, palms facing upwards and fingers pointing inwards towards each other.

2 Now inhale and stretch up out your body towards the ceiling, extending your spine and chest but keeping your shoulders down. Keep stretching until you feel the stretch over the outside of your wrists and forearms.

3 Breathe out and lean to the right, allowing your left elbow to bend. Feel the stretch deepen over the outside of the right wrist and forearm. Inhale, stretch up to the middle, exhale and lean over to the left, bending the right elbow and stretching the left wrist and forearm. Repeat this exercise twice.

INTRODUCTION

GETTING STARTED

BALANCING & STANDING

FLOOR POSTURES

WORKOUTS MADE EASY

RELAXATION

If you get wrist strain after doing the Downward Facing Dog (see page 41) and Crow (see page 76) poses, this exercise will help to ease it out.

INTRODUCTION

GETTING STARTED

BALANCING & STANDING

FLOOR POSTURES

WORKOUTS MADE EASY

RELAXATION

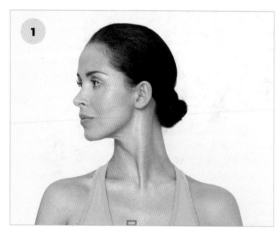

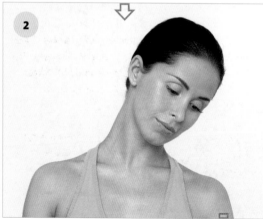

WARM UP YOUR NECK AND SHOULDERS

We all tend to suffer from tension in our neck and shoulders, and these easy exercises will increase flexibility, tone up your muscles and ease out any stiffness. You can do them at any time, even at work if you need to relax after a long session in front of the computer screen or before you go to bed to release the tension of the day.

Neck stretches

1 Sit with your back straight, shoulders relaxed, looking straight ahead with your chin parallel to the floor. Turn your head as far as it will go to the right without moving your shoulders. Now turn it to the left. Repeat 5 times on each side.

2 Now, without moving your shoulders, drop your head to the right as far as it will go – keep looking straight ahead. Come back to centre and then drop your head to the left. Repeat 5 times on each side.

3 Drop your head forward towards your chest, without moving your shoulders. Then lift it up towards the ceiling, stretching the front of your neck. Repeat 5 times.

4 Drop your head down and roll it gently round to the right and then continue circling it until you come full centre again. Repeat 5 times and then roll it in the other direction 5 times.

Move your head gently until you feel a deep stretch in the opposite direction to the way the head is going. The head is a heavy weight, and neck stretches need to be done carefully.

Breathing exercises

► ► ► Before you start your yoga session, take some time to sit quietly and practise your breathing. Although we breathe naturally all the time, we tend to breathe in a shallow way and aren't conscious of our breath. Yogic breathing teaches us to breathe deeply and strongly, and to harness the power of breathing to boost the flow of energy in our bodies and focus inwardly. Here are three techniques to get you going.

Alternate nostril breathing

1 Sit up straight in the Easy Pose (see page 32) and just breathe slowly and rhythmically. Bend the index and middle fingers of your right hand over into your palm, keeping the other fingers and thumb straight.

2 Press your right thumb against your right nostril and inhale slowly and deeply through the left nostril. Take a full breath, then press the fourth and little finger against the left nostril and gently exhale out fully through the right nostril.

3 Pause at full exhalation and repeat again, inhaling through the right nostril and exhaling out the left side. This cycle of breath should be repeated a minimum of 3 cycles or eventually practised for 1–2 minutes.

4 As you build your breath capacity, you can try to inhale for 6 counts, hold the breath for 6 counts and exhale for 6 counts. You can then build this up to 8, 10 and then, 12 counts.

Zest tip

Alternate nostril breathing helps to open the nasal passages, so is good if you are suffering from any breathing difficulty. Start slowly and build up gradually.

INTRODUCTION

GETTING STARTED

BALANCING & STANDING

FLOOR POSTURES

WORKOUTS MADE EASY

RELAXATION

INTRODUCTION

GETTING STARTED

BALANCING & STANDING

FLOOR POSTURES

WORKOUTS MADE EASY

RELAXATION

Ujjayi breathing

1 Stand tall with your spine straight, knees slightly bent, hips tucked under and your hands in the prayer position in the middle of your chest.

2 Inhale deeply through your nose and back of the throat, creating a 'Sa' sound, and bring your arms out to the sides at shoulder height, palms facing upwards. Keep your shoulders down and elbows slightly bent.

3 Inhale until your lungs are full and your ribs are fully extended outwards, pulling your stomach in. Hold the breath for 2–3 seconds and then exhale fully, making a 'Ha' sound and bringing your hands back to the prayer position. Repeat 10 times.

Zest tip

Ujjayi breathing is about learning to breathe into the back of the throat and making a full breath. The arm movements will help to encourage your chest and lungs to open.

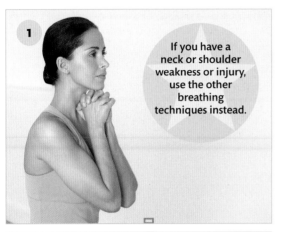

If you have a neck or shoulder weakness or injury, use the other breathing techniques instead.

Accordion deep breathing

1 Stand with your feet hip-distance apart or with your toes and heels touching. Interlace your fingers and lower your chin onto your knuckles. Keep the knuckles and the chin together throughout the breathing.

2 Keeping your spine straight, tailbone tucked in and elbows close together, inhale through your nose and raise your elbows up towards the ceiling as your chin gently presses into your knuckles. Keep inhaling until your lungs are full and ribs extended. Hold the breath for 2–3 seconds.

3 Exhale with your mouth wide open, lifting your head up and backwards, using your knuckles. Drop your shoulders down and bring your palms, wrists, forearms and elbows together, up and off your chest. When you reach full exhalation, hold for a couple of seconds before inhaling again. Repeat the full breath 10 times.

Zest tip

This breathing creates a stretch in the neck and should also strengthen it, if you keep the chin and knuckles connected and create resistance as the chin comes down on the inhale.

INTRODUCTION

GETTING STARTED

BALANCING & STANDING

FLOOR POSTURES

WORKOUTS MADE EASY

RELAXATION

Sun salutations

▶ ▶ ▶ This flowing sequence of yoga postures is a great way to start the day. The Sun Salutations warm and tone your body, building core strength and making your spine more flexible. Invigorating yet calming, they will boost your energy levels for the busy day ahead. Go with the flow and start right now.

1 Prayer pose
Feet apart to hip distance and standing tall, exhale slowly and deeply with your hands pressed together in prayer at chest height.

2 Back bend
Inhale slowly and deeply and stretch your arms up over your head with your thumbs crossed and palms open, gently dropping your head back and arching your spine from the waist. Your hips should be

forward and your neck relaxed, with firm legs, knees slightly bent.

3 Forward bend
Now exhale, pulling in your stomach muscles. Gently fold over forwards with bent knees and a flat back, placing your fingertips in line with your toes until, eventually, your palms are flat on the floor.

4 Easy lunge
Inhale, looking straight ahead and chest up. Move your right leg straight back until your right knee is on the floor, toes tucked under and then lift your chest further.

INTRODUCTION

GETTING STARTED

BALANCING & STANDING

FLOOR POSTURES

WORKOUTS MADE EASY

RELAXATION

5 Easy plank

Exhale, step your left leg back until both knees and toes are down on the floor. Inhale with your chest forward and your weight over your hands and toes. Your hands should be directly under your shoulders, with palms flat and fingers spread out. Keep your head and body in a straight line. Now exhale, gently bending your elbows and lowering your body towards the floor.

6 Cobra

Inhale and push your hands into the floor, extending your legs and pointing your toes with feet open to hip distance. With your hips and stomach still touching the floor and elbows bent backwards and pressing in, lift your chest and look forwards.

7 Downward facing dog

Exhale, curling your toes under with your feet hip-distance apart. Now raise your hips and create an inverted 'V' shape with your body and legs. Pull in your ribs and core muscles to support your back, and try to gently stretch your heels into the floor. Take 5 breaths in and out.

Downward facing dog: If your heels are more than 2cm (1in) off the floor, take a wider stance. If your shoulders are stiff, open your hands more and turn the fingers slightly outwards. If your hamstrings are tight, keep your knees slightly bent.

8 Easy lunge

Inhale and look straight ahead. Step your right leg forward, placing your foot between your hands with your left knee resting on the floor. Now lift your chest a little more.

9 Forward bend

Exhale, pulling in your stomach muscles, and step your left leg in until the toes of both feet are in a line. With your feet apart, gently fold forwards, bending your knees slightly. Let your head and neck drop. Your weight should be over your toes.

10 Back bend

Inhale and stretch your arms up over your head, palms open and thumbs crossed, while gently dropping your head back, looking back, arching your spine from the waist. Your hips should be forward and your neck relaxed.

11 Mountain pose

Exhale and bring your arm back down to your sides. Stand tall, stretching up through your body, and then relax. You're now ready to face the day!

INTRODUCTION

GETTING STARTED

BALANCING & STANDING

FLOOR POSTURES

WORKOUTS MADE EASY

RELAXATION

Advanced sun salutations

▶ ▶ ▶
As you progress with your yoga practice, your body will feel stronger and more flexible. You may wish to introduce new challenges into your familiar sequences and push yourself further. If you've already mastered the basic poses on the previous pages, why not take the plunge and make it a little harder?

This more advanced version will test your strength and suppleness, so give it a go. More experienced yoga practitioners can do the Sun Salutations with their legs and feet together.

Listen to your body

If you find these postures too difficult at first, don't worry. Just go back to the previous routine on pages 40–41 and work at the postures until you feel confident, comfortable and physically ready to move

forwards. Listen to your body – it will tell you when you are ready to take the next step. Don't try and rush it. Yoga is about the journey, not the finish line, so take all the time in the world and enjoy the ride.

1 Prayer pose

Feet together and standing tall, exhale slowly and deeply with your hands pressed together in prayer mudra (see page 124) at chest height.

2 Back bend

Inhale slowly and deeply and stretch your arms up and back over your head with the thumbs crossed and palms together, gently dropping your head back and arching your spine from the waist as you lift the chest upwards. Relax your neck and push your hips as far forward as possible, with firm legs.

INTRODUCTION

GETTING STARTED

BALANCING & STANDING

FLOOR POSTURES

WORKOUTS MADE EASY

RELAXATION

3 Forward bend

Now exhale, pulling in your stomach muscles. Gently fold over forward, keeping your legs straight if your back is strong enough (if not, keep your knees bent), placing your fingertips in line with your toes until, eventually, your palms are flat on the floor.

4 Lunge

Inhale, looking straight ahead and chest up, so the back is flat. Exhale, step your right leg straight back and then lift your chest further.

5 Plank

Exhale and move your left leg back until both legs are together with your knees off the floor. Inhale and create a straight line with your body, extending through the top of your head and heels. Pull up the tops of your thigh muscles and firmly pull in your stomach to support your back.

6 Lowered plank

Exhale, bend your elbows in and back and extend your breast bone forward while lowering your body down halfway. Note: do not let your chest go below elbow height. Inhale and extend forward, rolling over your toes into Upward Facing Dog.

7 Upward facing dog

With your legs and pelvis off the floor and feet together, extend through your toes as you look up, lifting your chest upwards. Keep your arms straight

and shoulders down, with your shoulder blades pulled in and down.

8 Downward facing dog

Exhale, curling your toes under with your feet closer together and your heels closer to the floor. Lift your hips and create an inverted 'V' shape. Pull in your ribs and core muscles to support your back, and gently stretch your heels into the floor.

9 Forward bend

Inhale and jump in – or walk one foot and then the other in – until your toes are in line between the hands. Gently fold forwards, bending your knees slightly. Let your head and neck drop until your weight is over your toes.

10 Back bend

Inhale and stretch your arms upwards, gently dropping your head back and arching your spine from the waist. Your hips should be forward and your neck relaxed.

11 Mountain pose

Exhale and return to the centre, bringing your arms back down to your sides. Stand tall, stretching up through your body, and then relax.

> If you have hyper-extended elbows, keep them a little bit bent to strengthen the muscles around the elbow joints.

INTRODUCTION

GETTING STARTED

BALANCING & STANDING

FLOOR POSTURES

WORKOUTS MADE EASY

RELAXATION

INTRODUCTION

GETTING STARTED

BALANCING & STANDING

FLOOR POSTURES

WORKOUTS MADE EASY

RELAXATION

These three postures from the Sun Salutation sequence work on similar principles of alignment, so focus on these points and master the poses. The same principles can be used in Mountain, Easy Plank, Easy Lunge, Lowered Plank, Reverse Triangle (see page 59) and Bridge (see page 94).

★ Internal rotation of the thighs
★ Core strong (stomach muscles and ribs pulled in, except in Bridge)
★ Shoulders down to lengthen the neck
★ External rotation of the upper arms.

With any posture where weight is over the palms, like Downward Facing Dog or Plank, make sure that the index finger, thumb and inside wrist joints take the pressure. These points are stronger and make a triangle that will support the upper body more easily.

Lunge

Engage the stomach and keep the ribs pulled in – this will help to lengthen and strengthen the spine. The bent knee should be directly over the ankle or foot to support this joint. Keep both legs internally rotated and pull up on the thigh muscles. Remember to place the hands under the shoulder, with palms flat, fingers spread outwards, middle index finger pointing directly forwards.

Plank

Toes press down into the floor as the heels push away. The thighs are rotated inwards and thigh muscles are strong. Keep the stomach muscles and ribs pulled in to support the core and the back. The back should be straight! The neck remains in line with the spine, so keep the shoulders down and upper arms rotated outwards.

Downward facing dog

Press the heels into the floor, keeping the thighs rotated inwards and pull up the thigh muscles. The tailbone points upwards, as the stomach muscles and ribs are pulled in. It is important to keep the shoulders down away from your ears and externally rotate the upper arms, otherwise you can create a great deal of pressure in the neck and shoulders. Remember to keep the palms flat, fingers spread outwards, middle index fingers pointing directly forwards.

Child's pose

▶▶▶ This restful pose can be used to calm and relax the body and the mind. It's great for easing tension and loosening up your body before you start your yoga session, during the class to re-energise or for chilling when you feel worn out after a busy day of work.

★ It stretches out your spine, hips, thighs and ankles.
★ It increases blood flow to the front of the body and brain and normalises circulation.
★ It brings instant relief when you are feeling tired or stressed.

1 Kneel on the floor, keeping your body and back straight, with your heels tucked under your bottom. Let your arms hang down by your sides. Move your legs together until your knees and ankle bones are touching each other.

2 Breathe in slowly and stretch up through your body from your buttocks to the top of your head, opening your chest as you do so. Then exhale and lean forwards over your knees, rolling down slowly and extending your spine until your forehead is flat on the floor and your chest is resting on your thighs.

3 Move your arms back so the palms are resting on the floor, face up or down, or on the soles of your feet. Breathe normally and focus on relaxing your head, neck and back. Hold the posture for 1 minute and then slowly roll up back into the starting position.

Variation: Open the knees to allow the chest space and extend the arms forward, palms facing down.

You can do this resting pose between other yoga postures to stretch out and relax your body. To make it more comfortable, you can rest your head on a cushion or folded blanket. If you are pregnant or have knee problems, ask your yoga teacher for advice before attempting it.

Balancing & standing

Just as you need balance and harmony in your life, especially if you have a very busy lifestyle juggling home and work commitments, you need to balance your body. Yoga can be very beneficial in achieving this, especially the standing poses, which will help improve your posture and make you feel fresher and more alert. This chapter shows you the most important poses, so relax, change into some comfortable clothes, pick a quiet spot and start practising now.

1 Mountain

▶▶▶ This basic pose looks so simple and natural and it's one of the most important ones to learn as it aligns your body and is the foundation of all Hatha Yoga postures.

★ It improves your posture, helping you to stand tall, feel better and look slimmer.
★ It tones and firms your stomach and arm muscles.
★ It builds support for the spine and joints and creates full body awareness.
★ It improves circulation and stimulates energy flow in your body.
★ It helps develop balance and stability.
★ It's relaxing and calming, helping you to breathe more deeply – so what are you waiting for?

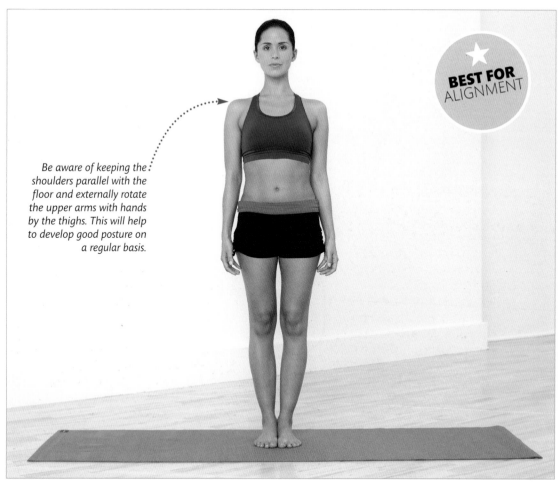

★ **BEST FOR** ALIGNMENT

Be aware of keeping the shoulders parallel with the floor and externally rotate the upper arms with hands by the thighs. This will help to develop good posture on a regular basis.

INTRODUCTION

GETTING STARTED

BALANCING & STANDING

FLOOR POSTURES

WORKOUTS MADE EASY

RELAXATION

The body structure should remain the same as with the shoulders down – ribs and stomach pulled in, hips neutral, thighs engaged and feet grounded to the earth.

Zest tip

To maintain good alignment, think: neck long, shoulders down, ribs and stomach pulled in, hips tucked under, thigh muscles engaged and feet side by side.

INTRODUCTION

GETTING STARTED

BALANCING & STANDING

FLOOR POSTURES

WORKOUTS MADE EASY

RELAXATION

1 Stand up straight and tall with your feet together or hip-distance apart, flat on the floor, toes spread out and feet parallel to each other. Your arms should hang comfortably at your sides, nice and relaxed, and your legs should be firm. Your hips should be level, pointing forwards, with your thighs turned slightly inwards – this helps stabilise your spine.

2 Relax your shoulders downwards, and pull in your ribs and stomach. Feel your spine lengthening as you do so, from your tailbone right through to the top of your head. Try to imagine you are pulling your spine up by a piece of string.

3 With your eyes open or closed and chin parallel to the ground, breathe slowly through your nose. Focus on your breath, holding it for 30 seconds and then building up to 1 minute.

4 When you are able to do Mountain pose naturally, inhale and raise your arms to the side and upwards, palms facing in. Exhale, keep the shoulders down, inhale and stretch the fingers towards the ceiling. Exhale and release the arms to the side of the body. Repeat several times.

2 Standing camel

▶▶▶ Back bending helps to open the front of the body and bring energy inside as you stimulate the spine and nerves. This supported back bend uses gravity to help open up your chest and stretch your spine, preparing you for the rest of your class.

★ It stretches out your neck, shoulders, chest and abdomen.
★ It makes your spine more flexible.

INTRODUCTION

GETTING STARTED

BALANCING & STANDING

FLOOR POSTURES

WORKOUTS MADE EASY

RELAXATION

Pull your elbows in towards each other to open your chest.

Remember to ground down into your feet.

Put your hands on your buttocks to support yourself as you open the front of the body.

Zest tip

When you do this posture, remember to focus on stretching and opening the front of your body instead of just leaning back. To help you do this, think about creating space in the front of your body and opening your heart!

If you suffer from a stiff or sore neck and shoulders, don't drop your head back! Simply look up and try to open your chest more and develop a stronger lower and middle back bend.

Bring your feet closer together as the bend becomes easier.

INTRODUCTION

GETTING STARTED

BALANCING & STANDING

FLOOR POSTURES

WORKOUTS MADE EASY

RELAXATION

1 Stand with your feet hip-distance apart or even wider if you have stiff hips or need to feel more stable and balanced. Check that your feet are parallel with each other and pull up your thigh muscles. Place your hands on the back of your buttocks with your palms facing forwards and fingers pointing downwards, thumbs facing out. Relax your shoulders down and pull in your elbows towards each other to open your chest.

2 Take a deep breath and gently drop your head back, looking back as far as possible. Get used to the feeling of stretching and opening the front of

your body. Inhale again and lift your chest upwards. As you exhale, gently deepen the back bend by pressing your hips more forward and letting your head go even further back.

3 At the deepest opening, try to hold the pose and simply breathe and be still for 10 or 20 seconds, depending on how strong you are and how long you've been practising yoga.

4 Inhale and release back out of the position the way you went in. As you progress and it gets easier, try to bring your feet closer in.

YOGA MADE EASY   **51**

3 Wide-leg forward bend

▶▶▶ This is good for loosening up and reducing muscle tension and stiffness. It stretches the muscles in the back of the legs, hips and spine. Even if you're not very supple and find it hard to bend forwards from your hips, just go as low as you can and keep working on this pose. Remember, the body will open up with practise.

★ It strengthens your leg muscles, toning your thighs.
★ It boosts circulation and helps digestion.

INTRODUCTION

GETTING STARTED

BALANCING & STANDING

FLOOR POSTURES

WORKOUTS MADE EASY

RELAXATION

Stretch up through your spine to the top of your head as you inhale.

Pull in your bottom and lift your chest.

Try to keep your legs straight, kneecaps pulled up and thigh muscles engaged and rotated internally.

★
BEST FOR
WARMING UP LEGS AND HIPS

Rest your hands on your thighs or place your hands on your hips and bend forward. This depends on the strength of your back.

Feel your spine stretching out as you lower your head and raise your bottom.

If you have a bad back, head or neck problems, take extra care and ease yourself in very gently. If it feels uncomfortable, stop immediately.

If your lower back is weak, you can bend your knees as you lower your body forward. Then, with your hands on the floor, straighten your legs.

Use your hands and forearms to stabilise you. If your head cannot reach the floor, walk your feet out a little more, with your weight on your arms.

INTRODUCTION

GETTING STARTED

BALANCING & STANDING

FLOOR POSTURES

WORKOUTS MADE EASY

RELAXATION

1 Stand up straight with your feet together and flat on the floor, your arms hanging at your sides. Move your feet wide apart – about 1.4m (4½ft) – keeping them flat on the ground with toes pointing forwards.

2 Inhale deeply and stretch up through your spine to the top of your head, lifting your chest and pulling in your bottom.

3 Exhale and gradually lower your upper body forwards from the hips until you are parallel to the floor with your arms straight below your shoulders and palms flat on the ground.

4 Breathe in and walk your palms back inside your feet, then breathe out and bend your elbows back as you slowly push your head down to touch the floor. Feel your spine stretching out as you gradually lower your head and raise your bottom. Don't rush this – go as far as you can and take your time.

5 Inhale and gradually reverse out of the posture, a little at a time, until you are back in the vertical starting position.

4 Warrior II

▶▶▶ This is a great all-round way to stretch out your body and open your hips, pelvis and thighs. A core posture, the Warrior will make you feel stronger, more empowered and give you that feel-good factor that yoga addicts love. Warrior II comes before Warrior I in this book because most students find it easier to achieve.

★ It improves circulation and blood flow around your body.
★ It opens up your chest, helping you to breathe more slowly and easily.
★ It improves your balance and boosts your stamina.
★ Feel the stretch in your groin and inner thigh muscles.

1 Stand with your feet approximately arm-span distance apart (or as far as possible without feeling uncomfortable or awkward), heels in line. Keep your feet parallel to each other. Keep your arms relaxed at your sides, hands resting lightly on your hips. Turn your right foot outwards to 90 degrees.

2 Now that your feet and legs are in position, hands on hips, exhale slowly, gradually bending your right knee until it forms a 90-degree angle, and keeping your body centred. If you need to adjust your feet, that's fine – the rest of your body will feel better if your legs and feet are aligned properly.

3 Keeping your hips down and forward, take a deep breath and start extending your arms upwards and outwards until they reach shoulder level. Make sure your arms are parallel with the floor. Keep your palms facing up. Your shoulders should remain down and relaxed. Don't rush this – just stay calm and relaxed and lift your arms smoothly and slowly. Turn your head slowly to the right. Breathe calmly and deeply and hold the position for 15 seconds.

4 Now inhale and slowly release yourself, lowering your arms and reversing out of the posture. Ease back gently into the starting position, so that you are facing forwards. Relax and then repeat on the other side.

Zest tip

As you practise and become more experienced and confident, you will eventually be able to extend your arms and legs at the same time to set up the posture.

INTRODUCTION

GETTING STARTED

BALANCING & STANDING

FLOOR POSTURES

WORKOUTS MADE EASY

RELAXATION

If you can keep your shoulders down and your upper arms externally rotated, then turn your palms down and maybe try a mudra hand position (see pages 124–125).

As your body gets stronger, you can hold this pose for longer.

The back arm should be directly in line with the front arm to create a line of energy and proper alignment. You should feel as if the arms are being stretched apart.

Keep your hips down and forward as you raise and extend your arms.

Try to ground the outside blade of the back foot into the floor and pull up the thigh muscle to create greater stability in the back leg.

The front knee should be directly over the ankle to support this small joint. In the beginning you might need to take a smaller step, so that your hips are higher up, but your knee is properly aligned.

INTRODUCTION

GETTING STARTED

BALANCING & STANDING

FLOOR POSTURES

WORKOUTS MADE EASY

RELAXATION

5 Extended right angle

INTRODUCTION

GETTING STARTED

BALANCING & STANDING

FLOOR POSTURES

WORKOUTS MADE EASY

RELAXATION

▶▶▶ This yoga posture stretches out your whole body and is really useful for strengthening and toning your legs and keeping them in shape. You place one knee at a right angle (90 degrees) to the direction you're facing.

★ It helps ease out your lower back, especially if it's stiff or painful from driving or sitting for too long at your computer.
★ It stretches out your groin and hamstrings.
★ It opens your chest, helping you to breathe more easily.

Turn your eyes and head upwards and look into your left palm.

★ BEST FOR SIDE STRETCHING

If your legs still need to strengthen and your hips need to open, try using a block, or your upper body will collapse.

Keep trying to extend and expand through the fingers and outside blade of the back foot.

Externally rotate your thighs, keeping your hips forward, stomach in, and twist the upper spine back to open the chest.

Beginners:
If you need to adjust your feet, bring your hands to your hips and make the adjustment, then resume the position. The body will remain more stable this way.

Reach your arm to the right, stretching as far as feels comfortable.

1 Start by standing up straight with your feet together, arms at your sides. Step your feet out to the sides – about 1.2m (4ft) apart – and turn out your right foot at right angles to your body. Turn your left foot slightly inwards, heel away.

2 Now breathe in deeply and, hands on hips, slowly bend your right knee, keeping your hips down and creating a 90-degree angle with your leg. Lower and extend your body to the right – still facing forwards – and place your right hand on the floor behind your right foot (or use a block). Press your left hand into your lower back (sacrum) to open your chest and stack the shoulders one on top of the other.

3 Inhale and lift your left arm above you and over your head, reaching and stretching over your ear

as far as feels comfortable. Feel the stretch as you reach further and further over to the right. If the neck feels fine, then turn your eyes and head upwards and look into the centre of your left palm. Hold for 10, 20 or 30 seconds, breathing deeply and fully.

4 Inhale and slowly reverse out of the posture, gradually straightening your right leg and returning to step 1, then repeating on the other side.

Variation: Place your bottom hand and arm on the inside of the foot, so that your elbow rests against your knee. This gives support to the knee and is more stable when working with knee or hip weakness.

INTRODUCTION

GETTING STARTED

BALANCING & STANDING

FLOOR POSTURES

WORKOUTS MADE EASY

RELAXATION

6 Triangle

▶▶▶ This is a good all-round posture that works on different parts of your body – stretching, toning and strengthening. Keep practising and you will soon notice the difference it makes.

★ It tones your leg muscles.
★ It is good for balance and a flexible spine.
★ It strengthens your lower back and tummy muscles.

INTRODUCTION

GETTING STARTED

BALANCING & STANDING

FLOOR POSTURES

WORKOUTS MADE EASY

RELAXATION

Look up at your left hand and focus on your breathing.

Beginners: rest your hand on your shin to support the opening of your chest, and stretch your arms in the opposite direction.

Make sure that your shoulders remain stacked on top of each other and your chest is open. As your legs and hips open, you will gradually be able to reach your hand to the floor.

The legs create the triangle shape, so make sure your step is big enough and that the base of your body is stable.

Use the extra stability of the reverse triangle to twist the spine further, keeping your legs firm.

Zest tip

When you do this exercise, make sure your shoulders and hips always stay parallel to each other. Imagine that your whole body is resting against a wall.

Reverse triangle: place your fingers on the outside blade of your foot.

INTRODUCTION

GETTING STARTED

BALANCING & STANDING

FLOOR POSTURES

WORKOUTS MADE EASY

RELAXATION

1 Stand with your feet wide apart with your right foot pointing out at right angles and your left foot turned in slightly towards the right. Breathe in deeply and raise your arms, so they are stretching out to the sides at shoulder level.

2 Exhale as you stretch over to the right, as if you were being pulled by your fingers. When the left side is fully extended, slide your right hand down your extended right leg to your shin, and extend your left arm straight up above you, palm facing forwards.

3 As you keep stretching even further to the right, lower your right hand as far as it will go, and look up at your left hand. Keep your hips pointing forwards all the time. Focus on your breathing

and hold the position for 10, 20 or 30 seconds. Inhale and then slowly reverse out of the posture back to your original starting position. Repeat to the other side.

Variation: Reverse Triangle. Begin as in Step 1, then exhale and twist your upper body to face backwards. Inhale and pull your stomach in, exhale and stretch through your left arm and fingers until your right side is fully extended. Then gently slide your left hand down your right shin. Inhale and place your right hand against your lower back (sacrum) and twist your upper body back, eyes up to the ceiling. If you can maintain the position comfortably, inhale and extend your right arm up over the left. Keep breathing, holding the posture for 10, 20 or 30 seconds then reverse out and repeat on the opposite side.

INTRODUCTION

GETTING STARTED

BALANCING & STANDING

FLOOR POSTURES

WORKOUTS MADE EASY

RELAXATION

7 Warrior I

▶▶▶ This important standing pose will help you to develop better core awareness, so you can really get to know your body and find your own inner strength.

★ It improves your sense of balance.
★ It strengthens and creates flexibility in your arms, legs, ankles, feet and knee joints.
★ It boosts your stamina and concentration.
★ It helps you breathe more deeply and fully.

Keep your head pointing forward for less pressure on your neck. Keep your shoulders down and stretch up through your fingers.

Think about stretching up through your fingers and down through the hips to create more expansion in the body.

Keep your thigh parallel to the floor.

Press the outside blade of your foot down and pull up on your thigh, with the thigh internally rotated.

INTRODUCTION

GETTING STARTED

BALANCING & STANDING

FLOOR POSTURES

WORKOUTS MADE EASY

RELAXATION

BEST FOR INNER STRENGTH

Advanced: bring your palms together, gently drop your head back and look up.

Zest tip

It's hard to keep your back foot flat on the floor if your legs are too far apart – move them in a little if necessary.

Feel the stretch in your back and neck as you drop your head.

Keep your extended leg straight.

1 Stand on the left side of the mat, feet together and arms hanging loosely at your sides. Step your right foot about 1.5m (5ft) to the right, turning your right foot out to 90 degrees and left foot into a 45-degree angle. Align both heels.

2 Exhale and rotate your body round to the right – it should be facing the toes of your right foot. Exhale and bend your right knee forwards over your right heel with your thigh parallel to the floor, keeping your left leg straight and extended behind you, and both feet flat on the floor.

3 Now take a deep breath and lift your arms straight up above your head, shoulder-width apart. Keep your face forward or, for a more advanced posture, bring your palms together. Drop your head back and look up, stretching out your back and neck. Breathe normally and hold the position for 30 seconds. Inhale and lower your head back to its normal position, then gradually reverse out of the posture, back to the starting position, and repeat on the other side.

INTRODUCTION

GETTING STARTED

BALANCING & STANDING

FLOOR POSTURES

WORKOUTS MADE EASY

RELAXATION

8 Crescent moon

▶▶▶ This standing pose is very similar to the one on the previous pages and is great for developing and improving your balance, co-ordination and concentration. Practise and see for yourself!

★ It opens up your chest, heart and hips.
★ It strengthens your legs, back, arms and shoulders.
★ It increases energy flow.
★ It stretches out the front of your neck, chest and hips.

Make sure the toes of your front foot point forward and your knee is over your ankle.

Keep your back knee down with your toes tucked under.

When you stretch out your arms, you also stretch your spine. Check with your yoga teacher if you have any back pain.

Inhale and lift your heart up to the ceiling. Bring your eyes and head back and then your arms. If your neck is stiff or weak, your head can remain more upright.

Keep your shoulders down and your shoulder blades pulled in to open up your chest.

BEST FOR
HIP
OPENING

Feel the stretch all over
the front of your body.

You are trying to create a full
spine back bend, so your lower,
middle and upper back should
be worked. Your hips can drop
forward as your arms reach
back further.

Straighten your back leg
to increase the stretch.
You can release yourself
at any point by dropping
the knee down.

INTRODUCTION

GETTING STARTED

BALANCING & STANDING

FLOOR POSTURES

WORKOUTS MADE EASY

RELAXATION

1 Stand in the Mountain pose (see pages 48–49) and place your hands on your hips. Inhale and take a big step forward onto your right leg, placing your right foot flat on the floor with the toes pointing directly forwards. Your left knee should be resting on the floor below you with the toes of your left foot bent and the left heel facing upwards. Bend the right knee to create a 90-degree angle with the right leg – your knee will be directly over the ankle. Keep your hips down and forwards, thighs rotated inwards. Now stabilise your feet and legs so you are well balanced, with your back leg acting as the main support.

2 Take a deep breath and bring your hands together in the prayer position in front of your heart. Look forward, inhale again and drop your head back.

Look back, fixing your gaze. Make sure you keep your shoulders down and shoulder blades pulled in to open up your chest. Lift your arms over your head and raise your heart upwards. Exhale and let your arms and head go back even more to increase the back bend. Feel the stretch all over the front of the body.

3 When you feel confident and balanced in this position, breathe in and extend your back leg straight. Breathe deeply while you hold this pose for 10, 20 or 30 seconds, as your yoga improves.

4 You can release yourself at any point just by dropping your back knee down to stabilise your balance and reversing out the way you went in. Repeat on the opposite side.

YOGA MADE EASY   **63**

▶▶▶ This pose will really test your balance and powers of concentration. Don't get disheartened if you can't do it first time – keep working at it and you'll succeed eventually. If you find it difficult wrapping at the wrists and bringing your palms together, don't worry – use a strap between your hands and work them closer together.

★ It strengthens your ankles and calves and stretches them out.
★ It stretches the upper back, shoulders, hips and thighs.

INTRODUCTION

GETTING STARTED

BALANCING & STANDING

FLOOR POSTURES

WORKOUTS MADE EASY

RELAXATION

Keep your abdominals engaged to strengthen the core muscles and create greater balance.

Zest tip
If you have problems wrapping your foot around, you can wrap at the knees, bending your bottom leg and resting your big toe on the floor. When your hips, knees and ankles open, you'll find it easier to wrap the foot around.

Squeeze your ankle against the back of the calf and your knees together in the middle, bringing more body weight into your heel. This will protect your knees by aligning your knees over your foot.

Concentrate on making your left leg stable and strong.

Twisting at the elbows and wrists will help to improve the circulation to the joints and help to open the shoulders and neck.

Cross your hands and wrists, thumbs facing you, and bring your palms together. If this is difficult, interlace your fingers, squeeze the palms together and then release your fingers.

Pull in your stomach muscles and lift your chest as you inhale.

INTRODUCTION

GETTING STARTED

BALANCING & STANDING

FLOOR POSTURES

WORKOUTS MADE EASY

RELAXATION

1 Stand up straight with feet together and arms by your sides, then bend your knees and lower yourself slightly into a sitting posture. Raise your right foot and bring your right leg over your left one, crossing them at the knees. Now point your right toes down and back and move your foot behind your left ankle, so it hooks behind your lower left calf muscle. You are now balancing on your left leg – hopefully. Concentrate on making your leg stable and strong.

2 Stretch out your arms parallel to the floor and lower your shoulders. Bend your right elbow and hook your right arm underneath and then over the top of the left elbow with your left arm bent. Lift both your forearms in front of you close to your body, with the backs of your hands facing each other.

3 Point your thumbs towards your face and your little fingers away from you. Now move your right hand in towards your face and cross your hands, so the palms meet. Interlace your fingers and pull down. Try to bring your palms together, then release your fingers.

4 Breathe in deeply and pull in your stomach muscles, lifting your chest. Breathe out and lower your elbows slightly to open up your shoulders. As you do so, 'sit down' a little lower if you can. Breathe gently and hold this position for 10, 20 or 30 seconds, depending on how experienced you are. Release yourself from the posture the way you went in and then repeat on the other side.

►►► Beginners may find this pose quite challenging, but it is also very calming and will help you develop good posture as well as better balance. You need strong knees and ankles to hold this position – balancing on one leg and not toppling over – but practise will make perfect, so just keep on trying and see for yourself.

★ It improves body co-ordination and balance.
★ It strengthens your ability to focus and concentrate.

Keep the core muscles engaged to create a stronger link between the top and bottom halves of your body.

Press the sole of your foot against your inner thigh, so you feel an opposite force. This will help you to balance.

Shoulders and hips should be parallel to the floor, pelvis tilted under and forward.

INTRODUCTION

GETTING STARTED

BALANCING & STANDING

FLOOR POSTURES

WORKOUTS MADE EASY

RELAXATION

1 Stand up straight, feet together and flat on the floor, arms relaxed and hanging down at your sides. If you need more stability to balance, place your left hand on your left hip. Bend your right knee and lift your right foot up and inwards, so the sole is resting against your inner left thigh. Move it higher until the heel is as high as it will go and pushing into the thigh, with your toes pointing down towards the floor.

2 Keep your supporting left leg firm and straight, tailbone tucked under and forward, so your hips are parallel with the floor. The right knee will open outwards. Inhale and gently bring your palms together in front of the heart centre, in prayer mudra (see page 124).

3 Take another deep breath and lift your arms straight up above your head with your palms touching each other. Keep stretching up through your body and hold this position as long as you can. Focus on your breath and relax into the posture. You may find it helps you to balance if you concentrate on a fixed spot in front of you.

4 Now lower your arms and ease back down to the starting position. Breathe normally and then repeat on the other side.

You need to focus on your core and really feel centred and rooted when you do this posture, or you will just collapse and fall over. Concentrate on your breathing and the vertical axis running right through the centre of your body.

Zest tip
Once you are able to balance well, try your hands in different mudras or stretch your arms out to the side.

Keep stretching up through your body.

Make sure your leg is firm and straight.

INTRODUCTION

GETTING STARTED

BALANCING & STANDING

FLOOR POSTURES

WORKOUTS MADE EASY

RELAXATION

Half moon

▶▶▶ This pose helps you improve your balance as well as making your legs and spine stronger. It targets your hips, thighs, buttocks and stomach as it tones your back, making you more flexible – it's a great standing pose.

★ It makes your hips and groin more mobile and stretches hamstrings, calves and shoulder area.
★ It improves digestion and helps release stress from the whole body.

Extend your left arm up as far as you can.

Try to fully engage your stomach muscles, as this will help you keep balanced and stable in the pose. It will also tighten the waist area.

If you have poor balance and find this position too difficult, do it with your back against the wall for support, or you can use a brick or block to support your lower hand.

Keep your foot firmly grounded into the floor and pull your thigh muscle up to keep your leg strong and stable.

INTRODUCTION

GETTING STARTED

BALANCING & STANDING

FLOOR POSTURES

WORKOUTS MADE EASY

RELAXATION

Lift your eyes to the ceiling and turn your head to face up.

Your shoulders need to be stacked one on top of the other, as if you were pressed against a wall.

Raise your left leg until it forms a straight line with your left hip, and stretch it out as far as it will go.

Keep your right leg straight.

INTRODUCTION

GETTING STARTED

BALANCING & STANDING

FLOOR POSTURES

WORKOUTS MADE EASY

RELAXATION

1 Stand up straight with your feet together and your arms hanging at your sides. Step your right foot out to the right – about 1m (3ft) – and turn your right foot out to a 90-degree angle, with your left foot turned in slightly. Stay facing forwards.

2 Inhale and raise your arms to shoulder height, then lower your right arm down towards the floor, bending your right knee. Keep lowering it until your fingertips are resting on the floor (or use a block). Keep your body and head facing forwards.

3 Breathe in and lift your leg up until it forms a straight line with your left hip. Be sure to keep your knee and toes facing forwards. Stretch out

your left leg as far as it will go as you straighten your right supporting leg.

4 Place your left hand on your sacrum (base of your spine), opening your chest and bringing your left shoulder over your right shoulder. Inhale and extend your left arm up as far as you can. When balancing well, lift your eyes to the ceiling and turn the head to face up. Hold this position for 10, 20 or 30 seconds, breathing normally. Then slowly ease yourself out of the position, bit by bit – don't rush it – until you are standing in the starting pose. Breathe slowly and deeply and then repeat to the other side.

12 Warrior III

▶ ▶ ▶ The last of the three variations of the Warrior pose (see also pages 54–55 and 60–61), this is another great posture for improving your balance and making your body stronger.

★ It strengthens your legs and ankles as well as your shoulders and back muscles.
★ It tones your abdomen.

INTRODUCTION

GETTING STARTED

BALANCING & STANDING

FLOOR POSTURES

WORKOUTS MADE EASY

RELAXATION

Try to keep your raised leg, arms and head parallel with the floor.

Keep your foot firmly grounded into the floor and pull your thigh muscles up to keep your leg strong and stable. Both thighs should be rotating inwards.

Point your toes downwards and out as if you were pressing into a wall.

★ BEST FOR STRONG BALANCE

Stretch your left heel backwards.

Zest tip

If you're a complete beginner, use a wall for support while you work on this and improve your balance. Either rest your raised foot against it or place your outstretched fingers on it – whichever is easier.

Inhale and contract your stomach, exhale and stretch your leg back until parallel with the floor. Keep your toes and knees pointing downwards.

INTRODUCTION

GETTING STARTED

BALANCING & STANDING

FLOOR POSTURES

WORKOUTS MADE EASY

RELAXATION

1 Stand up straight, feet together and arms resting by your sides. Breathe in and then bring your arms over your head, palms facing inwards and stretching out through your fingers in Mountain pose (see page 49). Pull in your stomach muscles to support your back.

2 Breathe out and step your right leg forward. Fix your gaze on a point on the floor about 1m (3ft) in front of your right foot. Make sure your foot is planted firmly on the ground with both your thigh muscles pulled up and your thigh bones rotated inwards.

3 Now stretch your arms and fingers forwards, as you lower your body until it is parallel with the floor. Simultaneously raise your left leg, stretching

your left heel backwards. Point the toes downwards and out to open your foot as if it was pressing into the wall behind it. Hold the final pose for 30–60 seconds, breathing gently through your nose.

4 Exhale and slowly step back and release out of the posture. Repeat on the opposite side.

Important: Try to keep your hips pointing directly downwards and your arms, head and lifted leg parallel with the floor. Your standing leg is the base of the balance, so keep it straight and pull up on the muscles above your knee, so you don't topple over.

13 Standing bow

▶▶▶ This pulling pose boosts blood flow to your heart and lungs and makes you feel really alive, transferring your circulation from one side of your body to the other and equalising it. If you practise this regularly you will become more flexible as your body opens and strengthens, and eventually you'll be able to do a standing split, with both legs straight up and down.

★ It expands your ribcage.
★ It tightens and tones your upper arms, hips and buttocks.
★ It makes your lower back more flexible.

Zest tip
If you find it hard to grab your foot on the inside, tightly grip the outside instead, with all your fingers together.

Keep your chin and eyes up, to help create a deeper opening in the chest and upper back.

Keeping your knees together to begin with will help to stabilise the hips and create stronger alignment.

Hold your left foot around the ankle with your fingers together.

INTRODUCTION

GETTING STARTED

BALANCING & STANDING

FLOOR POSTURES

WORKOUTS MADE EASY

RELAXATION

Maintain a firm grip on the ankle so that, as you kick back, your legs will open more, making the stretch deeper.

Keep stretching through the front fingers and back toes as if you were a bow that was being pulled apart.

This pose is quite challenging and you may find it difficult if you're just starting out in yoga. But put in the effort and, in quite a short time, you'll reap the rewards as your body becomes more supple and postures like this more within your grasp.

INTRODUCTION

GETTING STARTED

BALANCING & STANDING

FLOOR POSTURES

WORKOUTS MADE EASY

RELAXATION

1 Stand up straight, feet together, arms hanging relaxed at your sides. Find a spot on the wall in front where you can focus to help you balance. Transfer your weight onto your right leg, keeping it straight, and pull up the muscles above the knee to make the whole leg firm. Now bend your left knee and move your left heel against the buttock.

2 Bend your left elbow, keeping it tucked into your body, and reach behind you with your left hand, palm facing outwards. Lower your left arm and grab your left foot from the inside, holding it around the ankle with your fingers together. Raise your right arm, fingers together and palm facing forward. With your knees touching, concentrate on pulling up the muscles in your right thigh. Breathe in deeply and stretch up as far as possible. Without moving your head, try to touch your shoulder to your chin.

3 Lower your body forwards while strongly kicking back and up to create a deep back bend. Try to get your stomach parallel to the floor as you kick and stretch at the same time. As you kick back even further, your left foot should rise over your head even further into the bow and your left shoulder will be behind the left one. Stretch your right shoulder and arm in front of you until it is in line with your left shoulder. Your chin will rest on the shoulder with your fingers through the mid-line of your eyes. Try holding this position for up to 30 seconds at full extension.

4 Release yourself by kicking back against your hand and reversing out of the posture the way you went in. Stand still, breathe normally and then repeat on the other side.

▶▶▶ This is a brilliant way of developing your balance and strength and stretching out your whole body.

★ It improves your concentration.
★ It stretches your ankles, thighs, groin, stomach, chest and shoulder muscles.

INTRODUCTION

GETTING STARTED

BALANCING & STANDING

FLOOR POSTURES

WORKOUTS MADE EASY

RELAXATION

Adjust the strap on your foot – it needs to be tight to create the resistance to stretch the body fully.

If you have a longer strap, you can hold the end and then rotate your shoulder and arm and walk the hands in.

★ **BEST FOR** CONCENTRATION

Zest tip
Rotate your thigh inwards to help open your hips and create more space across your upper body.

1 Stand up straight, feet together and arms relaxed at your sides, and gaze at a fixed point in front of you on the wall. Shift your weight onto your right leg, keeping it straight and pulling up through the muscles above the knee into your hip. Now bend your left knee, placing your left heel in towards your buttock.

2 Wrap a strap loop around your left foot, holding the strap in your left hand, with the palm facing outwards, so your left shoulder can open. Keep your elbow bent in and facing down. Breathe in as you lift your right arm up until your arm is against your ear, palm forward and fingers together, stretching upwards.

3 Take another deep breath and kick your left leg back behind you and up towards the ceiling, bringing your body forwards into a deep back bend. You'll find that there's now some slack in the strap, so, with your palm facing upwards, bend your right elbow down and then out to the right and rotate your shoulder until the elbow points up.

4 Inhale and lift your chest as you drop your head back and raise your left arm over your head to reach for the strap. Holding the strap in both hands, gradually move them closer to your foot, arching your spine even further and dropping your head back until it reaches your foot. Try to hold this position for several breaths at full stretch.

5 Now gently reverse out the same way you went in. Relax, breathe normally and then repeat on the other side.

Walk the hand towards the foot – eventually you will rest the foot on the forehead and have your hands together, holding your foot.

Take it further...

Eventually, as your supporting leg becomes stronger and the other leg more flexible, you will create a deeper back bend, and you can try this posture without the strap. The grip would be the same, palm facing outwards, but with your foot flexed. Grab the underside of your foot, from the outside.

INTRODUCTION

GETTING STARTED

BALANCING & STANDING

FLOOR POSTURES

WORKOUTS MADE EASY

RELAXATION

15 Crow

▶ ▶ ▶ Master this arm balance and you'll be well on the way to becoming more proficient at yoga. It looks more difficult than it is but, if you practise it regularly and ease yourself into the posture, you'll be surprised at what you can achieve. With your weight supported on your elbows, you need to breathe deeply and focus deeply.

★ It strengthens your wrists, arms and abdominal muscles.
★ It stretches out your upper back and opens your groin.
★ It improves your breathing and fine-tunes your powers of concentration.

Wrists and hands should be shoulder-distance apart. Spread out the fingers and palms to make a bigger surface area to balance on.

Come up high on your toes, so your body weight can transfer forward.

BEST FOR
UPPER BODY
STRENGTH

Start by lifting one toe or foot off the floor, and then the other. This takes practise – moving slowly and with your breath helps!

Keep your gaze forward and fixed to help you balance. If you feel your neck is overstrained, then back out of the pose.

Zest tip

If you find it hard lifting your feet off the floor to begin with, raise them up on blocks. This will help push your weight forward and make lifting easier. Don't be upset if you fall over the first few times you try this position – everyone does! Just put a cushion or folded blanket on the floor in front of you to soften your landing.

Your toes should be pointed and your hips up in the air, with the weight over your arms and hands.

INTRODUCTION

GETTING STARTED

BALANCING & STANDING

FLOOR POSTURES

WORKOUTS MADE EASY

RELAXATION

1 Stand up straight in the Mountain pose (see pages 48–49) and then squat down with your feet positioned a little wider than hip-distance apart and your heels up off the floor. Place your arms between your knees, shoulder-width apart and elbows bent, with your palms flat on the floor. Rest the backs of your upper arms against your shins, and your knees on your upper arms.

2 Choose a fixed point on the floor in front of you and focus on it. Take a deep breath and gently pull in your stomach before breathing out and coming up high on your toes. As you do so, ease your weight forward over your hands, pressing more weight into your inner knuckles. Try to

keep your body tucked in and heels and tailbone close together.

3 Now lift one foot off the ground, then the other and try squeezing your knees in against your upper arms – keep pointing your toes. Balance and breathe, holding this pose for 3 or 4 breaths. This will probably be all you can manage when you start doing the Crow, but over time, as your strength and stamina improve, you can progress to holding it for 30 seconds to 1 minute.

4 Reverse gently out of the posture, gradually lowering your feet to the floor. Slowly rotate your wrists to loosen them up and release any tension.

floor postures

Standing and balancing helps to open up the body with the aid of gravity. When you move to the floor postures, the body needs to work harder, so this is where the real yoga starts. The floor poses will help you build greater strength and flexibility of the back and spine and make you feel more grounded and secure. By the end you will feel refreshed, recharged and re-invigorated, so lie down on your mat and get started.

Cobra

►►► When you do this yoga posture, you are mimicking a snake rearing up as you lift yourself up out of your body, opening up your chest and compressing your spine. It's actually a very easy and comfortable way to stretch out your back.

★ This tones up your arms and tummy muscles.
★ It helps relieve breathing and digestive problems.
★ It makes your spine more flexible.

INTRODUCTION

GETTING STARTED

BALANCING & STANDING

FLOOR POSTURES

WORKOUTS MADE EASY

RELAXATION

Keep your elbows in close to your body, shoulders down, to help you open the chest more and lengthen your neck.

If you have a bad back or you're pregnant, skip this posture.

BEST FOR LOWER BACK STRENGTH

Move your head and eyes upwards to create more opening in the front of the body but, if this feels strained, keep your chin and eyes parallel to the floor.

Eventually your whole spine should be bending back, bringing your head towards your knees. Keep pressing into the floor with your hands.

If you have a weak back, do a little bit, release and build up flexibility with repetition and frequency. Never strain!

As you get more comfortable, open your knees wider and lift your feet as well as your body.

INTRODUCTION

GETTING STARTED

BALANCING & STANDING

FLOOR POSTURES

WORKOUTS MADE EASY

RELAXATION

1 Lie flat on your front with your forehead resting on the floor, arms by your sides, and legs together with pointed toes. Place your hands, palms down, beneath the shoulders, your fingers together. The elbows will come up over the wrists. Your arms should stay close to your body.

2 Breathe in and slowly lift your head, neck, shoulders and chest off the floor. Try to use your lower back strength to lift, but if you can't, then push your hands into the floor to help you, with your elbows tucked into the body.

3 Continue lifting, raising your chest and upper body but keeping your legs and hips on the floor. Lift your head and eyes up, stretching the front of

your neck gently. At the full lift, hold the pose and breathe slowly for 10, 20 or 30 seconds.

4 Gradually reverse out of the posture, lowering yourself back down to the floor. First your stomach, your ribs, then your chest, neck, chin and, finally, your forehead. Turn your head to the right and relax. Repeat again and release out and turn your head to the left.

Take it further... When you are able to create a deep backbend, try to open your knees wider. Inhale, push your hands into the floor and lift both your body and feet, arching your back deeply. Eventually you will be able to touch the soles of your feet to your forehead.

2 Locust

►►► This pose is important because it strengthens your back, legs and arms. It can feel challenging to begin with, but keep trying and build up your strength and stamina. It is sometimes called the Grasshopper Posture.

★ It makes the muscles in your back stronger, as it creates greater flexibility.
★ It stretches out tight thighs and firms the buttock muscles.
★ It relieves indigestion.

INTRODUCTION

GETTING STARTED

BALANCING & STANDING

FLOOR POSTURES

WORKOUTS MADE EASY

RELAXATION

If you have lower back pain or you're pregnant, avoid this posture.

Your toes should be pointed to help stretch the whole leg. Try to lift the foot above the middle of your head.

Rest your chin on the floor, with your throat stretched out.

Try and keep your elbows straight and down on the floor. This will help to stretch this area, which can suffer from repetitive strain.

Keep your hips down on the floor as you lift your leg.

By pulling your hands back, you will stretch and open the chest, shoulders and neck. If your neck feels relaxed, try looking up and back.

Zest tip

If this is too difficult to begin with, use a strap between the hands and keep your legs open, but eventually work towards bringing them together. Practise, practise, practise!

Keep your thighs inwardly rotated, so that your knees and feet face directly downwards.

INTRODUCTION

GETTING STARTED

BALANCING & STANDING

FLOOR POSTURES

WORKOUTS MADE EASY

RELAXATION

1 Lie flat on the floor, face downwards, with your arms by your sides, palms and shoulders down and legs together. Point the toes on your left foot and keep your right leg relaxed. Bring your chin forward so it is resting on the floor with your throat stretched and imagine that you are stretching out and lengthening your whole body from head to toes.

2 Breathe in and slowly lift your left leg up behind you, keeping your hips down on the floor. Hold for 10 seconds and then gently lower it back down to the floor and repeat to the other side with your right leg.

3 Rest your chin on the floor, with legs together, hips pressing down and toes pointed. Reach behind you and interlace your fingers behind your back. Inhale, pull the fingers towards your feet, as you lift your head, chest, body and legs up off the floor. Hold the pose for 10 seconds at maximum height, breathing deeply, and then exhale and release the pose. Repeat again.

3 Floor bow

▶▶▶ This back bend will make you more supple, flexible and open. The more you practise it, the more comfortable you'll feel and the higher you will lift. Back bending increases the body's energy and has lots of health benefits, too.

★ It expands your chest and helps relieve poor digestion.
★ It tones up arm and leg muscles.
★ It stretches out your spine, relieving tension and making your back muscles stronger.

Keep your wrists and elbows straight, so that they aren't strained. This is more of a kicking posture, so the hands hold you in as you kick.

If you have back problems, check with your yoga teacher before trying this out.

Hold your ankles tightly.

Raise your chest and shoulders up off the floor.

BEST FOR BACK MUSCLES

Grip just under your toes – this will allow the shoulders and chest to open deeper. Eventually, with your head back, you will be able to see your toes above you.

Stretch your head up to look at the ceiling.

INTRODUCTION

GETTING STARTED

BALANCING & STANDING

FLOOR POSTURES

WORKOUTS MADE EASY

RELAXATION

1 Lie flat on your front on the floor, your head facing to one side, with your legs and feet together and arms by your sides. Keep your body in a straight line.

2 Bring your chin forward. Resting it on the floor, bend your knees until your feet are above the backs of your thighs. Grasp your right ankle with your right hand from the outside, and your left ankle with your left hand from the outside. Hold tight! Breathe in deeply and lift your chin off the floor.

3 Inhale again and kick your legs back and up, as you hold your ankles behind you. Simultaneously, lift your head up further and raise your chest and shoulders off the floor. Stretch your head up to look at the ceiling (if your neck feels fine) and hold this position for 30 seconds, breathing slowly and

deeply. The only part of you touching the floor should be your abdomen.

4 Exhale and gently lower your body and legs back down, then let go of your ankles. Turn your head to the right and allow your heels to roll outwards. This will allow your neck, back and legs to fully relax. Breathe low and slow, then repeat again and finish by turning your head in the opposite direction.

Take it further... If your back and neck feel fine, move the hand grip up just under the toes from the outside, with all your fingers together. Hold on and kick the body off the floor. When you are in the pose, keep breathing and try to bring the knees closer in and allow your shoulders to open more as you drop the head back. When you are at your deepest back bend, hold the pose, breathe, and then exhale and release fully.

4 Forward stretch

INTRODUCTION

▶▶▶ This relaxing stretch will calm you down and chill you out. Don't worry if at first you can't reach all the way down to rest your head on your legs – just bend your knee, hold on and keep practising. As you become more flexible, you'll be able to stretch further forwards.

★ It promotes inner stillness and calm.
★ It stretches out your neck, back, hamstring and calf muscles.

GETTING STARTED

BALANCING & STANDING

FLOOR POSTURES

WORKOUTS MADE EASY

RELAXATION

Zest tip
Ease yourself smoothly and gradually into this posture, going with the flow. Don't bounce, just breathe!

Your back should be nice and rounded. This will compress the front of the body and throat, which is good for stimulating digestion, internal organs and body systems.

Hold tightly about 5cm (2in) below your toes and flex the foot back, as you extend through your heel. This will help improve the flexibility of the foot, ankle and calf.

Touch your forehead on your knee. You can bend your knee if you need to. Push your forehead into your knee to stretch the back of the legs further.

At first your back might be quite rounded but, over time, try to stretch and lengthen it more from the lower back to the crown of the head.

As your body opens and gets longer on the back side, your elbows can bend towards the floor.

INTRODUCTION

GETTING STARTED

BALANCING & STANDING

FLOOR POSTURES

WORKOUTS MADE EASY

RELAXATION

1 Sit up straight on the floor with your weight on your seat bones, shoulders parallel to the floor and arms by your sides. Extend your right leg and bend your left leg so the bottom of the foot rests against the inner right leg. Try to keep the left knee on the floor.

2 Keep the hips down and inhale and sit up straight. Interlace your fingers, stomach pulled in, twist to the right and exhale, rounding over the right leg. Touch your forehead on your knee (knee bent if needed) and flex your toes back, gripping underneath the ball of the foot.

3 Begin stretching your foot back, heel away and, as you exhale, gently push your forehead into your knee to stretch the back of the legs further. Your back will round and your stomach will compress.

Bend your elbows down when you feel ready, keeping your shoulders parallel to the floor. Hold for 10, 20 or 30 seconds and the deepest stretch and then release and repeat on the other side.

4 Bring both legs together in front of you and sit up. Inhale and stretch your arms upwards, pulling in the stomach muscles. Exhale and bring the body forward and grab the outside of the feet firmly, with all your fingers together. Bend your knees a little if it helps. Hold on and exhale, stretching the feet back and open, as you stretch your body across your legs.

Take it further... As your feet, legs, hips and back open, your legs will be fully stretched across the floor and your body across your legs. This takes time, so just keep working on it.

YOGA MADE EASY   **87**

5 Cow face

▶▶▶ If you're wondering how this posture got its name, the crossed legs resemble a cow's lips while the bent elbows look like the ears. This is a challenging pose if you're still a beginner, but it's worth working at and mastering as it improves posture and helps you breathe more deeply.

★ It stretches out your shoulders, arms, hips and ankles.
★ It strengthens your back muscles.

INTRODUCTION

GETTING STARTED

BALANCING & STANDING

FLOOR POSTURES

WORKOUTS MADE EASY

RELAXATION

Allow your bottom shoulder to relax down as you pull in your shoulder blade and point your elbow further down towards the floor.

Your right elbow should point directly up at the ceiling, your left elbow should point straight down at the floor.

Keep your heels close to your hips, with your hips grounded into the floor. This might be difficult at first. When your hips open more through practising other postures, this will feel easier.

★ BEST FOR SHOULDER AND HIP FLEXIBILITY

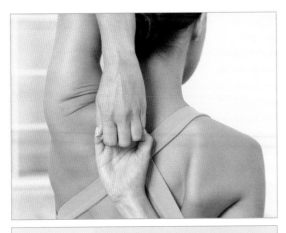

1 Sit up straight on your seat bones with your legs outstretched. Now bend your right leg in front and bring your right heel to rest on the outside of the left hip. Next, bend your left knee, crossing it over your right leg so your knees are stacked on top of each other and your toes are pointing backwards. Gently pull your feet in as close to your buttocks as they'll go.

2 Breathe in and, keeping your body upright, lift and extend your right arm straight out in front of you at shoulder height with your palm turned up. Keep raising it until it is vertical above your head.

3 Bend your right elbow and drop your arm down behind your back. Exhale and bend your left arm at the elbow behind your back and raise your left hand until it clasps your right hand behind your shoulder blades.

4 Hold this position, breathing rhythmically with your right elbow pointing straight up at the ceiling and your left one pointing straight down at the floor. The top arm should eventually be centred, behind the head. You should feel a nice stretch along the chest, underarm and shoulder.

5 Release your hands and reverse out of the posture back into the starting position, with your legs stretched out in front and arms at your sides. Repeat to the other side.

Use a strap if necessary and walk the hands closer together, until you can clasp the hands and hold on. Feel the opening in opposite directions, going up and downwards.

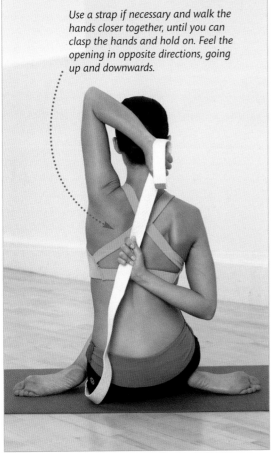

Zest tip
You can use a yoga strap if you can't reach far enough behind your back to clasp your hands.

INTRODUCTION

GETTING STARTED

BALANCING & STANDING

FLOOR POSTURES

WORKOUTS MADE EASY

RELAXATION

6. Pigeon

▶▶▶ This is a great hip opener, especially good if you spend your life sitting at a computer screen and your hips get tight and aren't very flexible.

★ It stretches your thighs and groin.
★ It relieves stiffness in the hip area.

★ It stimulates digestion.
★ It opens up your chest, shoulders and neck.

If you have an ankle, knee or hip injury, don't attempt this until you've fully recovered.

Remember to keep both hips pointing downwards, to help open them further. This area might feel tight at first, but keep practising and flexibility will come.

1 Rest on all-fours, with your knees directly under your hips, or begin in Downward Facing Dog (see pages 40–41). Exhale, and move your right knee forward behind your right wrist. Extend the right heel outwards away from your hips to create enough space for both hips to rest on the floor, or as close to it as you can manage. Stretch your left leg directly backwards, gently pointing your toes.

2 Exhale and gently slide your hands forwards until your head is resting on the floor, face down. (You can hold your elbows if this is more comfortable.) Breathe and maintain this pose for 30 seconds. Try to inwardly rotate your left thigh to open up your hips – your left knee should point directly towards the floor.

3 Press your left toes onto the floor and stretch them out to straighten your left leg even further, placing your hands back in the original position. Spread out your fingers with your index fingers pointing forward and centred. Breathe in and push your hands down, lifting your head and eyes up and back as you lift your chest. Keep your shoulders down and arms fully extended, without locking the elbows. Try to stretch out as far as you can through the front of your body. Inhale again and lift your ribcage and lengthen your waist, dropping your head even further back, while keeping your shoulders down. Breathe, remain calm and, when you are ready, release out the way you went in and repeat on the other side.

Take it further... When you can do the Pigeon at full stretch, you're ready to move on to the King Pigeon (see opposite).

INTRODUCTION

GETTING STARTED

BALANCING & STANDING

FLOOR POSTURES

WORKOUTS MADE EASY

RELAXATION

6b King pigeon

▶▶▶ When you move on to start practising the King Pigeon – a deep back bend – you'll need to use a strap around your ankle as it's quite a challenging position, but well worth the effort!

INTRODUCTION

GETTING STARTED

BALANCING & STANDING

FLOOR POSTURES

WORKOUTS MADE EASY

RELAXATION

Hold the strap as close to the foot as possible. When your chest, shoulders and front open, you will be able to work without the strap.

Use your hands and arms on the floor to help you balance and create grounding. If your hips are still tight, the tendency is to roll to the side.

Try to maintain a sense of resistance between the foot and the body to help you open up more. Imagine the foot pulling back and the chest and the body lifting and moving forward.

1 Begin by bending your left knee, and bring your left foot up over the knee, wrapping a strap loop around your left ankle or foot. Hold the strap with your left hand, palm facing outwards. Bend your left elbow down and then rotate the elbow out to the left and rotate and open your shoulder socket until the elbow is pointing upwards. This can feel quite strange at first!

2 Inhale and lift your chest, dropping your head back and lifting your right arm over your head as you reach for the strap. With both hands on the

strap, begin edging your hands closer to your foot, arching your spine and dropping your head back even further until your head and foot meet. Try to hold for several breaths at your deepest extension. Gently release out of this position the way you went in and then repeat on the other side.

Take it further... When your shoulders, chest, spine and hips are more flexible, try this without the strap. The grip would be the same – palm facing out and upwards, but with the foot flexed. Grab the underside of your foot, from the outside.

7, Hero

INTRODUCTION

GETTING STARTED

BALANCING & STANDING

FLOOR POSTURES

WORKOUTS MADE EASY

RELAXATION

▶▶▶ You can use this restful pose when you meditate as it's very grounding and calming. If, at first, you aren't supple enough to lower your bottom on to the floor between your feet, you can raise it up on a cushion or folded blanket. The more you practise, the more comfortable you'll feel.

★ It decompresses your knees and ankles.
★ It soothes aching, tired legs.
★ It stretches the thighs, hips and front of the body, especially when you fully recline.
★ It improves circulation in your feet and toes.

Keep your gaze forward or slightly down and soften your gaze, so your awareness becomes more internal.

Sit up straight if your knees feel comfortable.

If you have knee, hip or ankle problems, check with your instructor that this is safe for you.

Keep the body weight more over your fingers, if your knees feel very stiff. Take your time allowing the knees to open and hips to rest on the floor.

1 Kneel with your back straight and thighs, knees and ankle bones together. The tops of your feet should be resting on the floor and your toes extended straight back. Keep your shoulders and arms relaxed and press your buttocks down onto your heels.

2 Lean forward, lifting your hips slightly, keeping the weight over your fingers, and slowly move your feet apart to either side of your buttocks. Reach down and place your thumbs on the inside of the calves and gently roll the muscles outwards to create more space.

3 Put your fingers on the floor beside your ankles and breathe in deeply, stretching up through your spine to the top of your head and expanding your chest. Keep your eyes focused on a spot straight ahead of you. Lengthen your tailbone into the floor and relax your shoulders.

4 Now lean slightly forwards, so your buttocks gradually come to rest on the floor. Then gently sit up again if your knees feel comfortable. When your knees and legs open sufficiently, you can bring your hands into a mudra (see pages 124–125).

7b Reclining hero

▶▶▶ Don't attempt this variation until you feel relaxed in the sitting Hero pose. Your buttocks must be comfortably on the floor before you try to take the pose further.

INTRODUCTION

GETTING STARTED

BALANCING & STANDING

FLOOR POSTURES

WORKOUTS MADE EASY

RELAXATION

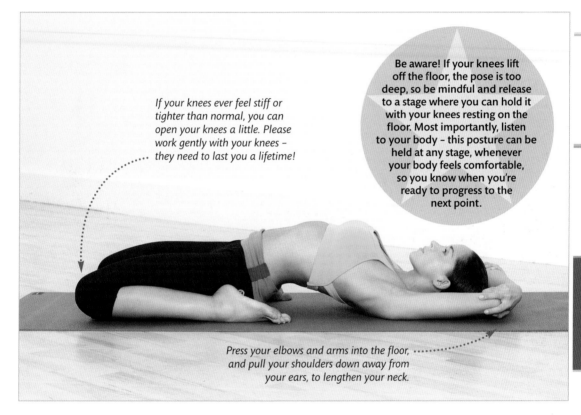

If your knees ever feel stiff or tighter than normal, you can open your knees a little. Please work gently with your knees – they need to last you a lifetime!

Be aware! If your knees lift off the floor, the pose is too deep, so be mindful and release to a stage where you can hold it with your knees resting on the floor. Most importantly, listen to your body – this posture can be held at any stage, whenever your body feels comfortable, so you know when you're ready to progress to the next point.

Press your elbows and arms into the floor, and pull your shoulders down away from your ears, to lengthen your neck.

1 With your buttocks resting comfortably on the floor, place the palms of your hands onto the soles of your feet or tops of your toes and take your weight into your elbows on the floor. If this feels comfortable, drop your head back, sliding your elbows gently forwards. When your body weight is supported on the floor, lift your arms over your head and grab your elbows.

2 Pulling gently on your elbows, lower the top of your shoulders away from your ears, pressing your chin into your throat and stretching out the back of your neck. If you are doing this correctly, you should be able to arch and lift your upper back in a strong back bend. Breathe gently and hold the position for 20–30 seconds, depending on how strong you are.

3 Release yourself carefully from the pose, reversing out slowly the way you entered it.

8 Bridge

▶▶▶ With this simple back bend, you can bridge the gap between your body and mind and discover your inner stillness. It's also a great way to energise and refresh your body.

★ It opens up your chest and the front of your body.
★ It massages and realigns your spine.
★ It strengthens your hips and legs, toning those thigh and buttock muscles.
★ It's a great way of relieving menstrual pain and tummy tension.

You can place a block between your knees to help keep them aligned with your ankles and maintain an inward rotation of your thighs. This will also help to tone your inner thigh muscles.

Push your hips and pelvis up towards the ceiling.

Place your palms under the small of your back to support the spine and create a greater opening over the front of the body.

When your back is stronger, raise the hips higher, with your palms facing inwards, fingers spread and pointing upwards.

If you suffer from back pain or knee problems, talk to a yoga teacher before trying this posture.

Your body weight should rest over your shoulders.

Try to gently press your chin into the throat, to open and stretch the back of your neck and upper back further.

INTRODUCTION

GETTING STARTED

BALANCING & STANDING

FLOOR POSTURES

WORKOUTS MADE EASY

RELAXATION

1 Lie flat on your back with your arms by your sides, palms facing downwards. Bend your knees, hip-distance apart, so your feet are flat on the floor, with your knees over your ankles and your fingertips close to your heels. Gently breathe in and out, watching your chest rise and fall.

2 Inhale deeply and lift your buttocks and thighs off the floor. Keep your feet flat on the floor and pull in, tightening your bottom and thigh muscles as you push your hips and pelvis even higher. Feel each and every vertebrae lift of the floor, one by one. Support the small of your back with your hands as your body weight rests over your shoulders. Breathe rhythmically for 30 seconds or so and then slowly return to the floor and the starting position.

2a Supported shoulder stand

INTRODUCTION

GETTING STARTED

BALANCING & STANDING

FLOOR POSTURES

WORKOUTS MADE EASY

RELAXATION

▶▶▶ When you start out, you'll have to do the supported version of this posture, but as you progress and become more accomplished, try the more advanced unsupported shoulder stand (opposite). It's surprisingly comfortable and relaxing and a good pose to include in your pre-bedtime routine, especially at the end of a stressful, tiring day.

★ It is calming and brings instant relief from fatigue.
★ It helps improve digestion.

★ It tones the muscles in your legs and buttocks.
★ It helps to lower the heart rate.

Zest tip
If your shoulders and neck are stiff, put a folded blanket or extra mat below your shoulders and upper back.

Have your palms and wrists firmly resting on your back to support the lift. Eventually you will move your hands to the upper back.

1 Lie on your back, chin on your throat, neck extended along the floor. Breathe out and roll onto your shoulders. As you bend your knees into your forehead, place both palms on the small of the back. Rest your elbows firmly on the floor, as close together as they will go, to give your back maximum support.

2 Inhale and stretch your feet upwards, at first with bent knees but then eventually stretching out your legs to their full extension. If you have trouble raising your legs, walk them up a wall until your arms can support them. Inwardly rotate your thighs, and keep stretching your toes and legs upwards from the base of your spine.

3 Breathe in and edge your elbows closer together, walking your hands down your back towards your shoulders. Gently press your shoulders, upper arms and elbows into the floor to support your middle back – this will allow you to stretch up even further.

4 Make sure you keep your head straight throughout the whole pose. Eventually your spine will be vertical at right angles with the floor. Hold this position as long as possible, breathing naturally. With practise, you can stay like this for up to 5 minutes.

▶▶▶ When you can stay comfortably in the Supported Shoulder Stand, you can move on to this more intermediate version. Just follow steps 1–4 on the facing page and then continue as follows:

BEST FOR CALMING

To support your back, keep the stomach muscles engaged. If your back begins to collapse, keep it supported with your hands until it gets stronger.

The body weight is balanced over the back of the head, neck and shoulders, so go into this pose slow and steady.

Place your hands against the thighs to create support, but keep stretching your toes upwards.

1 From the shoulder stand, tip your hips backwards and lower your legs to a 45-degree angle with your back slightly concave. Concentrate on your breath and, when you feel comfortable, gently remove your right hand from your back and place it on your right thigh. Do the same with your left hand, moving it to your left thigh – your palms should rest inwards against your legs.

2 Keep your legs straight and rotate your thighs inwards. Balance and breathe normally.

Eventually, when you can relax in this position, it will feel very comfortable.

3 Release out by placing one hand and then the other on the base of your spine, with your elbows on the floor. Gently lower your knees to your forehead and roll your spine slowly down.

INTRODUCTION

GETTING STARTED

BALANCING & STANDING

FLOOR POSTURES

WORKOUTS MADE EASY

RELAXATION

10 Fish

▶▶▶ This is a great way of opening up your chest and relieving any stiffness in your neck and spine. It can be very calming after a stressful day at work.

★ It stretches out your neck and spine.
★ It helps relieve breathing problems.
★ It tones your arm muscles.

INTRODUCTION

GETTING STARTED

BALANCING & STANDING

FLOOR POSTURES

WORKOUTS MADE EASY

RELAXATION

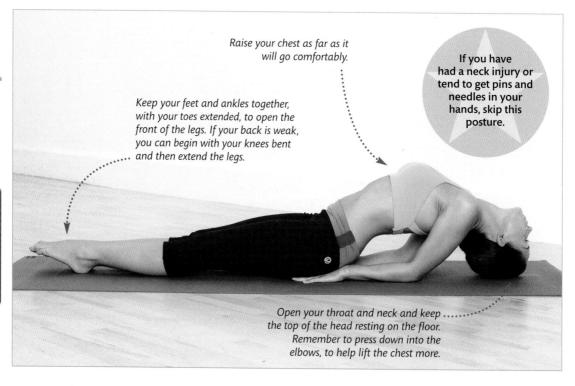

Raise your chest as far as it will go comfortably.

Keep your feet and ankles together, with your toes extended, to open the front of the legs. If your back is weak, you can begin with your knees bent and then extend the legs.

If you have had a neck injury or tend to get pins and needles in your hands, skip this posture.

Open your throat and neck and keep the top of the head resting on the floor. Remember to press down into the elbows, to help lift the chest more.

1 Lie flat on the floor on your back with your legs and feet together, arms by your sides, palms down.

2 Move your hands in, side by side, under your bottom, and take a deep breath.

3 As you breathe out, lift your chest, arching your back and pressing your elbows into the floor.

4 Keep lifting slowly, moving your head back until the top touches the floor and your chest is raised as far as it will go comfortably. Hold this position for 30 seconds, breathing slowly and deeply and focusing on your breath. Then reverse out of the pose, slowly lifting your head and lowering your body and sliding your arms back out to your sides.

Your legs and arms should be parallel with each other.

Place your palms together, with thumbs crossed if you need added support for the arms.

Keep your hips and head firmly on the floor.

INTRODUCTION

GETTING STARTED

BALANCING & STANDING

FLOOR POSTURES

WORKOUTS MADE EASY

RELAXATION

Take it further... If your back and stomach muscles are strong, then follow steps 1–4, and breathe in the posture. Inhale, your arms upwards with your palms pressing together. Keep your hips and head firmly on the floor. Exhale, pull the stomach muscles in and lift the legs upwards so that the arms and legs are parallel with each other. Hold the pose for 10, 20 or 30 seconds. Exhale and release the pose, first bringing your arms down to support your back and then your legs. Lift your head, slide your arms down and rest in Corpse pose (see pages 106–107).

11 Boat

▶▶▶ This balance posture will help you tone and strengthen your body and keep your waist nice and trim. It's quite challenging because you need a mixture of muscle strength, inner calmness and a good overall sense of balance to perform it correctly.

★ It strengthens your back, abdomen, hips and thighs.
★ It is uplifting and helps develop stamina and determination.

Place your palms, facing inwards, against your legs, keeping your arms parallel to the floor. This will help to create support and alignment for your body.

Keep your shoulders relaxed and down.

Keep your legs pressing together, and your toes pointed. This will help to strengthen and stretch the legs.

Skip this pose if you have a weak lower back. Or try it with the knees bent and hold for a few seconds until you build more back strength.

INTRODUCTION
GETTING STARTED
BALANCING & STANDING
FLOOR POSTURES
WORKOUTS MADE EASY
RELAXATION

1 Sit up straight on your seatbones with your shoulders parallel to the floor, arms at your sides and legs together, extended in front of you, toes pointed.

2 Take a deep breath and stretch up out of your waist, lifting your chest and extending your spine from the tailbone to the top of your head and pull in your stomach muscles.

3 Exhale and lean back to a 45-degree angle, lifting your legs straight up into the air in front of you, so

you are balancing on your seat bones. Your body should create an 'L'-shape. Keep your legs together, toes pointed, and lift your arms – one by one – to rest your hands against the outside of the thighs or knees. Hold the posture, breathing slowly. Keep your shoulders relaxed down as you stretch out your legs and spine.

4 To come out of the posture, slowly lower your legs and raise your upper body until you are sitting upright and let your arms drop to your sides. Repeat again and build your strength and stamina.

BEST FOR
STOMACH
STRENGTH

Fingers should be interlaced behind your head to support the head and neck. As the elbows move back, keep the shoulders down and try to keep lifting the chest upwards.

Keep the stomach muscles pulled in firmly to support the back and maintain a strong connection between the top and lower halves of the body.

Stretch your legs and spine up and out.

INTRODUCTION

GETTING STARTED

BALANCING & STANDING

FLOOR POSTURES

WORKOUTS MADE EASY

RELAXATION

Take it further... If your back and stomach feel strong, then follow steps 1–2. Exhale, stomach muscles pulled in, and lean back to a 30-degree angle, raising both legs up and balancing on your seatbones. Keep your chest lifted and then place one palm behind the head and then the other, fingers interlaced to support the head. Pull the elbows directly back, in line with the shoulders, to open the chest further. Keep breathing and stretch your spine and legs up and out. Hold for 10, 20 or 30 seconds, exhale and release the arms first to support the body, then bring your legs down gently.

Variation: You can also try this with your knees bent, feet parallel to the floor and palms besides the knees. This will take the pressure off the back.

INTRODUCTION

GETTING STARTED

BALANCING & STANDING

FLOOR POSTURES

WORKOUTS MADE EASY

RELAXATION

▶▶▶ Here are two easy yoga postures to make your back stronger and more flexible. These simple seated twists can bring relief to an aching back and help prevent future problems by restoring the back's natural flexibility. So what are you waiting for? Get going now!

★ They relieve tension in the spine and increase flexibility.
★ They strengthen the muscles supporting the spinal column.
★ They are good for digestive problems.

The elbow against the outside of the knee will create leverage and resistance to allow you to stretch deeper into the whole spine.

Zest tip
If this is difficult, wrap your right hand or elbow around the outside of your right knee and grab the side of your left knee. This twist is easier to achieve and, as you get more supple, you can advance to the technique below.

Keep your palm flat on the floor with the fingers facing away from your body.

Easy noose pose

1 Sit upright with your knees bent and feet flat on the floor, keeping your knees and feet together. Place your feet about 50cm (20in) in front of your buttocks. Place your left hand behind your back, with your palm flat on the floor and fingers pointing away from your body, supporting your back. If this is too difficult, just use your fingertips. Lift your right arm upwards and extend your arm and shoulder beyond your left knee, placing your fingers on the floor.

2 Inhale as you pull in your stomach and lift your chest, stretching your spine upwards. Now breathe out and rotate your head, chest and spine to the right. Repeat, twisting the whole spine even deeper from top to bottom. Do this 3 more times. Now reverse out and then repeat on the other side.

Zest tip

If you find this difficult, repeat steps 1,2 and 3, but in step 4 wrap your right hand around the outside of your left knee and grasp the side of your knee. Practise this until you're more flexible and then progress to the technique below.

Remember to keep the shoulders down, parallel with the floor, to lengthen the neck and twist more into the upper back.

Place the foot firmly on the outside of the knee and keep the knee bent, pointing directly upwards.

INTRODUCTION

GETTING STARTED

BALANCING & STANDING

FLOOR POSTURES

WORKOUTS MADE EASY

RELAXATION

Sage twist

1 Sit up straight, hips on the floor, and extend both your legs in front of you. Bend your left knee and place your left foot on the outside of the right knee, parallel with your right leg. Try to keep both hips on the floor. You may find it helpful to gently walk your buttocks back slightly so your hips and sitting bones are more evenly placed.

2 Place your left hand behind your back and rest the palms or fingertips on the floor, pointing them away from your body.

3 Lift your right arm straight up and bring the whole arm and shoulder beyond your left knee – gently push the knee back with your elbows and place your fingers on the floor or on your right knee.

4 Breathe in deeply, pulling in your stomach and lifting your chest as you stretch your spine upwards. Breathe out and rotate your whole body, then your head to the left. Inhale again and press your hands and hips down as you stretch up through the top of your head, lifting more through your lower back and twisting even deeper. Repeat 3 times, then reverse out and repeat on the other side.

Take it even further... If you're really super-flexible and an advanced yogi, you can try binding your arms through your legs and twisting deeper.

13 Reclining twists

▶▶▶ These relaxing twists are great for releasing tension and making you feel less stressed. A great way to end a yoga class or a stressful day. Try them and see for yourself.

★ They stretch out your spine and help relieve lower back pain.
★ They help to improve digestion and elimination.

★ They tone and slim your waist and hips.
★ They can be used in your warm-up routine.

INTRODUCTION

GETTING STARTED

BALANCING & STANDING

FLOOR POSTURES

WORKOUTS MADE EASY

RELAXATION

Place the opposite hand on the outside of the knee. This will help to ground the legs to the floor and keep the shoulders down, to enhance the twist.

Remember to keep your elbow and the back of the hand down on the floor to help keep the shoulders and chest open.

Zest tip

If your lower body is stiff, place a rolled blanket or block under your knees. This will decrease the intensity of the twist.

The extended hand should be in line with the shoulder. Try to look over the palm at the fingertips and soften the gaze.

If it is difficult to hold the big toe, try using a strap around the foot and keep extending around the foot until you can grab the toe.

Both shoulders should remain flat on the floor and down away from the ears to allow more space for the neck and chest.

★ **BEST FOR** SPINE FLEXIBILITY

INTRODUCTION

GETTING STARTED

BALANCING & STANDING

FLOOR POSTURES

WORKOUTS MADE EASY

RELAXATION

1 Lie on your back with the knees bent and feet flat on the floor. Have your arms by your sides and your shoulders and hips parallel to each other. Stretch out your arms at shoulder height on either side, with your palms upwards.

2 Keep your knees together and bring them up over the hips and flatten your lower back. Now breathe out and slowly lower your knees to the left, knees in line with the hips. Place your left hand on the right knee.

3 Keep both shoulders flat on the floor and turn your head to the right to look over the right shoulder. Bend the right elbow and point the fingers upwards. Hold the posture for 20, 30 or 60 seconds and breathe slowly. With every exhale, try to deepen the twist and stretch.

4 Now slowly bring your knees and head back to the centre and then repeat on the other side.

Variation: If you're feeling fit and supple, you can try some advanced versions of this posture with the legs extended. Instead of bending both knees, keep your right leg straight and left knee bent. Exhale and bring your left knee to the right and extend the arm fully. Keep the bottom leg fully stretched. Taking it further, extend both legs to create a 90-degree angle and clasp your big toe with the opposite fingers and twist the spine deeper.

14 Corpse

▶▶▶ Corpse pose (*shavasana*) is the classic relaxation pose. This might seem easy at first, but can be quite challenging to master, because you are required to do absolutely nothing except breathe.

INTRODUCTION

GETTING STARTED

BALANCING & STANDING

FLOOR POSTURES

WORKOUTS MADE EASY

RELAXATION

Corpse pose can be practised before a yoga session to relax the mind and body and become more centred, or at the end of a class to fully relax and allow the body time to process the benefits from the work you have done.

Shavasana can appear to be deceptively easy, but the challenge comes when you first try to lie still . The mind will start to think about all sorts of to-do lists, stresses and strains from the day, while the body will want to fidget, adjust your yoga outfit or move a hair from the face.

The key is first to relax the body and then the mind and begin to focus fully on your breathing. This is the reason why it is often easier to practise at the end of a yoga session, when the body has been stretched and the muscles relaxed.

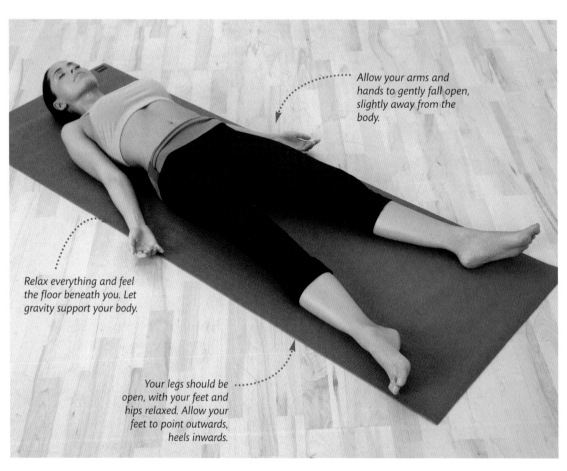

Allow your arms and hands to gently fall open, slightly away from the body.

Relax everything and feel the floor beneath you. Let gravity support your body.

Your legs should be open, with your feet and hips relaxed. Allow your feet to point outwards, heels inwards.

1 First of all, lie on your back and make sure that the body is symmetrical: the hips and shoulders are parallel, the neck is in line with the spine and the spine is straight, with the legs extended outwards. The legs should be open. Gently rotate the feet in and out to relax the legs and hips. When you feel comfortable allow the feet to remain pointing outwards, heels inwards. This will relax the hips and lengthen the lower back.

2 Now do the same with the hands and arms and let them gently fall open, slightly away from the body. This will relax the upper body, allowing the shoulders to drop down and the neck to lengthen, as the chest expands. You are trying to create more space in your body.

3 If it feels nice, gently roll the head from side to side and then bring it back to the middle. Imagine that someone is pulling the top of your head with a string to stretch and lengthen the neck and spine further. Tuck your chin down a little and close your eyes.

4 Now remember to relax everything! Feel the floor beneath you and let gravity support your body. As you breathe out, relax the feet, ankles and knees. Inhale and let the stomach lift, exhale and let the stomach fall and relax the legs, hips, stomach and chest. Breathe in and out again and fully relax the thumbs, wrists, arms, neck and head. Become aware of any leftover tension in the body and use your exhale breath to release it.

5 Your body should feel like it is melting into the floor – weightless and light. The mind should be relaxed, with a subtle awareness of your breathing. The inhale and exhale should be equal, especially at the end of a yoga session. Stay here for as long as you like. With practise you will be able to do Corpse pose for 10–20 minutes.

This is time for the body to recharge, rejuvenate and re-energise. The body, mind and spirit will start to become balanced and harmonised through space and time. Corpse pose trains you to release tension, experience a feeling of peace, to appreciate a sense of openness in the body and mind, and to learn the basics of meditation.

Notes

★ If you suffer from a weak lower back, place a rolled blanket or bolster under your knees – this will help to release pressure in the spine.

★ By placing clasped hands over the belly, you can learn to belly breathe. (This is the breathing done while in Corpse pose.) As you inhale, allow the stomach to rise and, with an exhale, the stomach should fall.

★ Corpse pose can be done on your front side, in between front-facing floor postures, if you require some time to relax. Simply turn the head to one side, allow the heels to turn out, feet turned in, with your palms facing up or interlaced under the face.

★ If the room feels cold, place a blanket over you, so you are not distracted by the temperature. You need to allow the body and mind to fully let go.

INTRODUCTION

GETTING STARTED

BALANCING & STANDING

FLOOR POSTURES

WORKOUTS MADE EASY

RELAXATION

Workouts
made easy

▶ ▶ ▶

The targeted workouts on the following pages will help you to make your yoga routine work for you. They have been specially designed to help solve common problems or to attain specific results. There is a sequence to perform at the office to help ease muscle tension and improve your posture in front of your computer, a sequence to relieve back pain, a sequence to prepare you for sleep, a sequence to tone and flatten your tummy and finally a 10-minute sequence to give you a speedy energy boost. If you make an effort to build these quick workouts into your daily life, you'll be astonished by the difference they can make to your health and wellbeing.

Office workout

INTRODUCTION

GETTING STARTED

BALANCING & STANDING

FLOOR POSTURES

WORKOUTS MADE EASY

RELAXATION

►►► If you spend long periods working at a desk or staring at a screen, your back and neck may start to ache and your posture will suffer. Performing some simple yoga exercises will calm and relax you.

Even while you're sitting down at work you can still stretch out your muscles and joints to ease away stiffness. Try our office workout to restore balance to your body, boot up your brain and give you the energy to carry on working. It only takes a few minutes.

Relax... just do it!
Alternate nostril breathing (see page 37) is a great way to calm down when you're feeling stressed and under pressure, and it helps develop concentration, too. Take time out from your work to breathe slowly and rhythmically before breathing through alternate nostrils, closing them with your thumb or fourth and little fingers. Do 3 cycles through both nostrils and you'll feel more relaxed.

Seated eagle
1 Sit on the edge of your chair and plant your left foot firmly on the floor. Lift your right knee and cross it over the left one. Point the toes of your right foot down, press your foot back and wrap your right ankle around the back of your left ankle.

2 Stretch out both arms in front of you parallel with the floor. Bring your right arm underneath the left and bend your arms at the elbows, pointing your fingers upwards, with your thumbs towards your face and the little fingers pointing away. Move your right hand in towards your face and cross your arms at the wrists, so the palms meet in the prayer position. If your palms are open, interlace your fingers and pull downwards.

3 Inhale as you pull in your stomach muscles and lift your chest to stretch out your spine. Exhale, lowering your elbows, as you squeeze your knees and ankles together. Hold for 3 breaths before releasing. Relax and breathe normally and then repeat on the other side. Do 2 repetitions on each side.

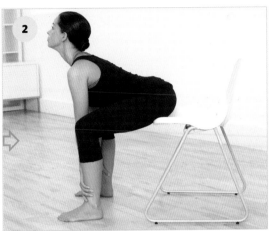

Forward/back stretch

1 Sit on the edge of your chair with your feet planted firmly on the floor wider than hip-distance apart. Breathe in and pull in your stomach muscles, then exhale as you lean forwards, tilting your pelvis forward. Place both hands around the inside of the ankles with your palms facing outwards. Press your

elbows in against your knees to keep them securely positioned above your ankles.

2 Inhale and arch your spine like an angry cat, stretching deeply into your back and pressing your chin gently into your throat as you look down at your chest. Exhale and raise your eyes and head, drop your shoulders down, pull in your stomach and lift your chest to arch your spine into a back bend.

3 At each full extension, hold the position for a few breaths, feel the deep stretch and then release. Sit still for a few breaths and then repeat the exercise twice.

Spinal twists

1 Sit on the edge of your chair with your feet hip-distance apart directly below your knees, with your palms resting on your knees. Inhale and pull in your stomach muscles and stretch your spine up, keeping the shoulders down.

2 Exhale and twist to the left, placing your left hand over the back of the chair and hold on. Place your right hand on your right knee. Inhale again and stretch up further. Exhale and twist more, bringing your body, head and eyes around.

INTRODUCTION

GETTING STARTED

BALANCING & STANDING

FLOOR POSTURES

WORKOUTS MADE EASY

RELAXATION

Banish back pain

INTRODUCTION

GETTING STARTED

BALANCING & STANDING

FLOOR POSTURES

WORKOUTS MADE EASY

RELAXATION

▶▶▶ Regular, gentle yoga sessions can help ease out an aching bad back as well as prevent future problems by strengthening and stretching your spine, making it more flexible.

Try our easy workout, specially for backs, and you'll soon feel the difference it makes. The postures work the full range of motion to really get your spine in gear. You may not be able to hold them for long initially, as you have to recondition your spine before stretching even further and deeper. If any of them start to feel painful, just back off, release out and then try again gently – don't go for the burn!

Back pain workout
★ Standing Forward Bend (this page)
★ Standing Half Moon (opposite)
★ Standing Camel (see pages 50–51)
★ Cobra (see pages 80–81 and note below)
★ Locust (see pages 82–83)
★ Standing Twist (opposite)

STANDING FORWARD BEND

Standing forward bend

1 Start off in the Mountain pose, feet open to hip distance, with your hands on your hips (see pages 48–49). Exhale, keep your stomach pulled in and slowly bend forwards from your hips, keeping your legs bent, but your back flat. As you lower yourself forwards, lengthen the front of your body.

2 Touch the floor in front of or beside your feet with your palms or fingertips, if you can reach down that far. Try grabbing your big toes with two index fingers. If you can't, place your palms on the back of your ankles or just cross your forearms, holding your elbows. As you do so, press your heels into the floor, try to straighten your legs and press the tops of your thighs inwards. Raise your sitting bones up and let your head drop down.

3 Hold for at least 30 seconds, gradually lifting and lengthening the front of your body as you breathe in, and releasing further into the forward bend as you breathe out. Release by raising your hands back up onto your hips, pulling in your stomach and bending your knees. Press your tailbone down and then lift the front of your body as you exhale.

> If you have a lower back weakness and find the Cobra difficult, try the Sphinx pose instead – it's a less intense back bend. Lie on your stomach, arms shoulder-width apart with elbows resting under the shoulders, and palms face down with fingers spread outwards. Keep your shoulders down away from your ears to help stretch your upper back, chest and neck. Lift your chest upwards as you look directly forwards – don't raise your head.

Standing half moon

1 Stand in Mountain pose (see pages 48–49) with your palms resting inwards against your thighs. Look directly forward with your chin parallel to the floor. Inhale and stretch your left arm up towards the ceiling, placing your elbow against your left ear, palms facing inwards. Inhale and engage your stomach muscles, grounding your feet into the floor, and stretching your fingers up even further.

2 Exhale and extend your right fingers and hand down your right thigh until you have a nice stretch over your left side. Hold at full stretch for 3 or 4 breaths, then inhale and lift back to the centre. Swap your arms and repeat on the other side. You can do this sequence twice if you wish.

Standing twist

1 Begin in Mountain pose (see pages 48–49), feet grounded down and thigh muscles pulled up. Place your right hand on your left hip. Inhale and stretch your spine up, keeping your shoulders down, and extend your left arm directly out in line with your right shoulder.

2 Exhale and bring your left arm back further and twist your lower, middle, upper back and head around to the right. At the deepest stretch, hold the pose and breathe. Reverse out and twist on the other side. Repeat twice on each side.

INTRODUCTION

GETTING STARTED

BALANCING & STANDING

FLOOR POSTURES

WORKOUTS MADE EASY

RELAXATION

STANDING CAMEL

STANDING HALF MOON

STANDING TWIST

Sleep-well workout

Sleep can get disrupted if your body and mind are full of stress and tension. Yoga helps to release the tension from a busy day and will prepare you for sleep, when your vital energy will be restored.

NECK EXERCISES

Yoga can help you relax before going to bed, calming your mind and body and making you feel restful and ready for sleep. Create your own routine, involving gentle breathing exercises and stretches as well as forward bends and reclining twists. Here are some suggestions. Try them and see what works best for you.

Wind-down workout
★ Easy Pose (see page 32)
★ Active breathing (see page 23) or alternate nostril breathing (see page 37)
★ Neck exercises (see page 36)
★ Cow Face (see pages 88–89)
★ Forward Stretch (see pages 86–87)
★ Seated Forward Stretch (opposite)
★ Happy Baby (below)
★ Reclining Twists (see pages 104–105)
★ Corpse (see pages 106–107)

Happy baby
This is great at the end of the day for stretching out your groin and tired back muscles. It's very calming and chilling when you feel stressed out.

HAPPY BABY

1 Lie on your back with your head resting on the floor. Breathe out gently and bend your knees, bringing your legs into your tummy, with your knees close to your shoulders.

2 Inhale and grip the outside of your feet, all your fingers together – if this is too difficult, use straps around each foot and hold the ends. Open your knees wider than your body and bring them gently down towards the floor.

3 With your feet facing upwards – as if standing on the ceiling – and your shins perpendicular to the

INTRODUCTION

GETTING STARTED

BALANCING & STANDING

FLOOR POSTURES

WORKOUTS MADE EASY

RELAXATION

floor, heels directly over your ankles, gently press your heels upwards and pull gently down on your feet to create resistance.

4 Breathe out and pull your thighs inwards and knees down as you try to stretch out your spine from your tailbone right through to the top of your head. Hold for 30 seconds to 1 minute, breathing gently. Release out by lowering your feet to the floor and then lie still and rest for a few breaths.

Seated forward stretch
Relax and ease away any tension in your back, neck and shoulders with this simple pose.

1 Sit kneeling with your heels and feet together and hips grounded into your heels. Inhale, raising your arms over your head and bringing your hands together in the prayer position (see page 124). Keep your chin parallel with the floor and elbows aligned with your ears.

2 Inhale and pull in your stomach muscles and ribs, stretching up through your fingers. Exhale as you move your body forward in a flat-back position, allowing your stomach muscles to engage and resist the downward action.

3 Touch your forehead on the floor and relax your neck and head. Breathe out slowly and extend even further through your arms, keeping them straight and palms together, and pressing your hips down on your heels. Breathe at the deepest extension and hold for 30 seconds to 1 minute. Inhale and reverse out of the posture.

If you have a weak lower back, position your legs and hips before walking your hands forward along the floor until your head is down and then bringing your arms into the prayer position. Release normally as this will help strengthen your stomach and back muscles, but, if it feels uncomfortable, just walk your hands out the same way you went in.

SEATED FORWARD STRETCH

INTRODUCTION

GETTING STARTED

BALANCING & STANDING

FLOOR POSTURES

WORKOUTS MADE EASY

RELAXATION

INTRODUCTION

GETTING STARTED

BALANCING & STANDING

FLOOR POSTURES

WORKOUTS MADE EASY

RELAXATION

Tummy toners

▶ ▶ ▶ Use the following breathing exercises and yoga postures to engage your body and mind, flatten your stomach and tighten your abdominal muscles.

BOAT

ABDOMINAL BREATHING

Repeat this exhale-inhale cycle once every couple of seconds about 10 times. Keep practising, gradually building up the number of cycles.

If your tummy is a bit flabby and needs toning, put aside some time on a regular basis to practise this workout. You'll soon see a difference!

Tummy toner workout
★ Abdominal Breathing (below)
★ Cat and Dog Tilts (opposite)
★ Leg Lifts (opposite)
★ Boat (see pages 100–101)
★ Fish (see pages 98–99), compressing and stretching the stomach muscles.
★ Simple Seated Twists (see pages 102–103)

Start with abdominal breathing
Teach yourself the technique of *kapalabhati* abdominal breathing – it strengthens your tummy muscles, improves digestion and really energises you.
NOTE: Do not practise *kapalabhati* if you are pregnant.

1 Sit in a comfortable position with your back straight. Clasp one hand inside the other and place them gently over the abdomen. Try to concentrate on this area as you breathe. Relax the mouth and jaw.

2 Inhale first and then exhale forcefully as you pump your hands against your lower abdomen, contracting the muscles and your diaphragm to push air fully out of the lungs. The inhale will happen automatically. Keep repeating as you build up the number of breaths. Try 10, 20 and then 30 cycles of breath.

3 Then release your hands and relax, so your stomach expands naturally and your lungs fill up with air as you inhale.

CAT AND DOG TILTS

The more you practise this, the stronger your stomach muscles will become and you'll be able to hold the posture for longer.

Cat and dog tilts

1 Start in a kneeling position with your hands flat on the floor below your shoulders. Breathe in and pull your tummy muscles upwards and inwards as you arch your spine and lower your chin. Hold, breathing normally, for a few seconds.

2 Breathe out and lower your tummy, abdominal muscles and spine towards the floor as you raise your chest and hips upwards. Hold and move your head and left shoulder towards your left hip. Hold for a few seconds and then reverse back to the centre and the start position, before repeating on the other side. Do 3 repetitions each side.

Leg lifts

1 Lie flat on your back, legs and feet together, with your arms straight and hands slightly under your buttocks to support your back, palms flat on the floor.

2 Point your right toes, then inhale, pulling in your stomach muscles, exhale and raise your right foot about 5–7cm (2–3in). Hold this position for up to 20 seconds, breathing gently through your nose. Release and repeat on the left side.

3 Now point the toes of both feet and inhale, pulling in your stomach muscles. With the backs of your hands supporting your buttocks, exhale and lift both legs off the floor together. Hold for up to 10, 20 or 30 seconds, breathing through your nose, and then lower as you exhale.

LEG LIFTS

INTRODUCTION

GETTING STARTED

BALANCING & STANDING

FLOOR POSTURES

WORKOUTS MADE EASY

RELAXATION

10-minute energiser

▶▶▶ This is a really useful, speedy workout when you're in a hurry and don't have time for a leisurely yoga session. It will energise your mind and body and set you up for the rest of the day.

INTRODUCTION

GETTING STARTED

BALANCING & STANDING

FLOOR POSTURES

WORKOUTS MADE EASY

RELAXATION

10-minute workout

★ Standing Breathing (this page)
★ Sun Salutations (see pages 40–43) – one set only
★ Chair Twist (opposite)
★ Then hands down into Easy Plank (see page 41)
★ And step into Easy Lunge (see page 41) or Crescent Moon (see pages 62–63)
★ Eagle (see pages 64–65) or Tree (see pages 66–67)
★ Half Moon (see pages 68–69) or Warrior III (see pages 70–71)
★ Locust (see pages 82–83)
★ Bridge (see pages 94–95)
★ Reclining Twists (see pages 104–105)

Standing breathing

Start your workout with a simple breathing exercise to refresh and focus your mind, and prepare your body for the sequence of postures to come. This helps build lung capacity and warms you up, creating heat inside your body.

1 Stand with your spine tall, knees slightly bent and hips tucked under. Your hands should be in the prayer position (see page 124) in the middle of your chest.

2 Now inhale deeply through your nose and the back of your throat and take your arms out to the sides at shoulder height, keeping your shoulders down,

STANDING BREATHING

CRESCENT MOON

At the beginning, this sequence might take longer than 10 minutes but, once you master the poses, use your breath to move through them in a flowing manner and quicken the pace.

CHAIR TWIST

elbows slightly bent and palms turned upwards. Breathe in until your lungs are full, your ribs are extended outwards and your stomach is pulled in. Hold this breath for a few seconds and then breathe out fully as you bring your hands back into the prayer position. Repeat this exercise, inhaling and exhaling 10 times.

Chair twist

1   Stand in the Mountain pose (see pages 48–49). Take a deep breath and lift your arms up, parallel to the floor. Place the palms together in the prayer position (see page 124) in the middle of your chest.

2   Exhale and bend your knees, lowering yourself until your thighs are parallel to the floor and hips are down. Lean slightly forwards over your thighs until your body forms a right angle with them.

3   Lower your tailbone a little further towards the floor, extending your lower back. Exhale, pull in your stomach muscles and twist over to the left, placing your right elbow against the outside of your left knee. Turn your head, look upwards, hold and breathe. Exhale back to the centre and then twist to the other side. Return to the centre, exhale and release out until you are standing with your arms at your sides.

BRIDGE

When you start the postures, breathe deeply and consciously through your mouth but, when this feels normal and automatic, close your mouth and breathe through your nose.

INTRODUCTION

GETTING STARTED

BALANCING & STANDING

FLOOR POSTURES

WORKOUTS MADE EASY

RELAXATION

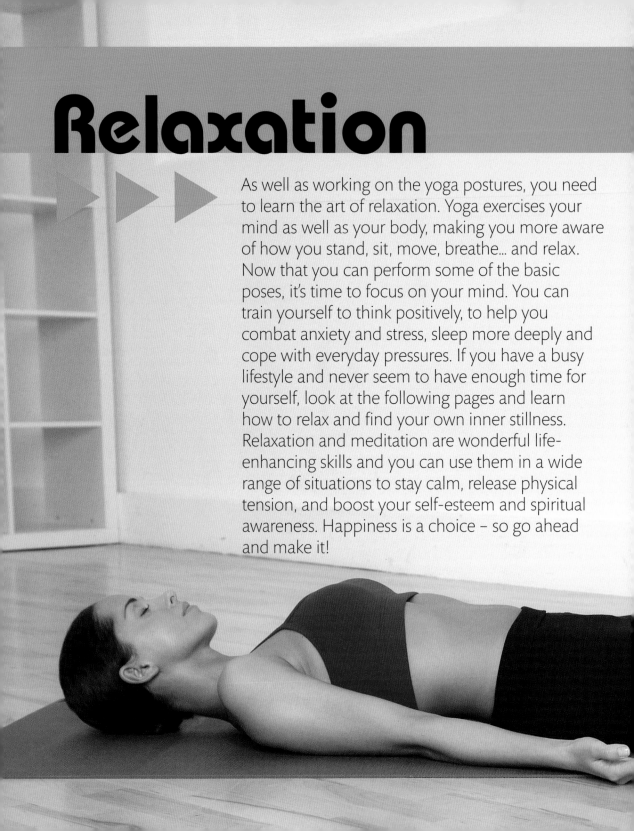

Relaxation

As well as working on the yoga postures, you need to learn the art of relaxation. Yoga exercises your mind as well as your body, making you more aware of how you stand, sit, move, breathe... and relax. Now that you can perform some of the basic poses, it's time to focus on your mind. You can train yourself to think positively, to help you combat anxiety and stress, sleep more deeply and cope with everyday pressures. If you have a busy lifestyle and never seem to have enough time for yourself, look at the following pages and learn how to relax and find your own inner stillness. Relaxation and meditation are wonderful life-enhancing skills and you can use them in a wide range of situations to stay calm, release physical tension, and boost your self-esteem and spiritual awareness. Happiness is a choice – so go ahead and make it!

Relaxation and meditation

INTRODUCTION

GETTING STARTED

BALANCING & STANDING

FLOOR POSTURES

WORKOUTS MADE EASY

RELAXATION

▶▶▶ When you're feeling tired, perhaps after a tough day at work, and your mind is still racing, how do your relax? Well, it's easier than you think. You just need to teach yourself some simple relaxation techniques and positions.

Get ready to relax!

You can prepare yourself for relaxation by breathing deeply (see pages 38–39) and sitting or lying down in one of the following positions – these will help release any tension in your body and make you feel calmer and more relaxed.

★ Chair sitting position (see below)
★ Easy Pose (see page 32)
★ Child's Pose (see page 45)– this is better as a relaxation posture.
★ Corpse (*shavasana*) (see pages 106–107)

Adopt whichever feels most comfortable and natural for you, and then concentrate on your breathing. Choose a point to focus on and draw inwards, moving on to breathing more deeply from the abdomen.

Move on to meditating

The secret of successful meditation is to start slowly and build up gradually – just like training your body, you can't rush it and expect instant results. Find a quiet place at home where you can sit still in a comfortable position. Sit in Easy Pose (see page 32) or just sit upright in a chair with your feet grounded on the

Above: Place blocks under your feet, if your feet don't feel grounded. The body's base should feel supported to allow the spine to sit upright.

Above: Hands in prayer is a great way to become more centred and connect the left and right sides of the body and mind.

floor. Make sure your head, neck and spine are all in a straight line. The good news is that practising the yoga poses in this book will strengthen your back muscles and improve your posture, making it easier for you to sit still for longer.

Now you are sitting comfortably, the next step is to become fully aware of your body and your senses: listen carefully, touch (perhaps hold a flower in your palms), see (focus on an object) and smell (burn some incense), and experience your body and your surroundings. Try to banish all other thoughts from your mind, breathe deeply and bring your full attention to the individual senses. Of course, this is easier said than done! Luckily, there are some techniques you can use to help you.

★ Focus on an object

Fix your gaze and concentrate on an object at eye level, such as a candle flame or even the tip of your nose. Fully experience the point of focus – this will help you to concentrate your mind more deeply and withdraw from your environment and physical senses.

★ Focus between the eyebrows

This sounds a bit odd but it works! Fix all your attention on a spot between your eyebrows and hold it until you can feel that spot intensely. Now close your eyes and keep focusing on that spot and breathe deeply. The mind will wander at first, but just keep bringing it back to the spot.

★ Be aware of your breath

Now that your mind is focused, it's time to become aware of your breath. Breathe slowly in and out through your nostrils. As you meditate, the rhythm of the breath will slow and become more even between each inhale and exhale. As you do this, thoughts may flow in and out of your mind but ignore them and just keep breathing steadily and focusing on the object you have chosen. If you set aside some time every day just to sit still and meditate, you will be surprised how easy it becomes – your powers of concentration and the space between thoughts will soon increase, and your mind will relax and be still.

INTRODUCTION

GETTING STARTED

BALANCING & STANDING

FLOOR POSTURES

WORKOUTS MADE EASY

RELAXATION

Corpse pose allows the body to fully relax, so you can begin to focus the mind on breathing and meditating. Keep your eyes open initially until you are meditating and then close the eyes and draw inwards, concentrating fully on your breath.

If you suffer from a weak lower back you can place a folded blanket under your knees to help release pressure in Corpse pose.

Mudras

▶▶▶ When you feel confident with yoga postures, alignment and breathing, try introducing mudras to increase the flow of energy around your body and create a deeper level of focus and calmness.

Mudras balance and heal your body and also lead to the higher awakening of the chakras (the seven main energy centres in your body along the spine) and kundalini (spiritual) energy. The mudras channel this energy, working on your mind as well as your body.

The most commonly known mudras are the hand ones – meditative gestures that help redirect *prana* (vital life force) back into your body. Each finger symbolises the energy of one of the planets, while the thumbs represent the ego (self). You can use them to focus your concentration, make you feel calmer, or fire up your body and mind, so you're more energised and ready for anything. Have a go and feel the difference.

Prayer (anjali) mudra

This neutralises the positive (male) and negative (female) sides of your body. You should always do this before starting your yoga class or practice at home. By pressing the palms of your hands together firmly, you connect the two hemispheres of your brain and bring them into balance. This is a great centring mudra.

Gyan mudra

Place the tips of your index finger and thumb together. The index finger symbolises the planet Jupiter, which represents knowledge and expansion.

Above: Prayer mudra can be used at the beginning of a class or simply as a greeting.

Above: Place a block underneath your buttocks if your knees feel stiff when sitting for longer periods of time.

This is one of the most commonly used mudras, helping to make you feel calmer and more receptive, as it purifies the mind and creates a sense of wisdom.

Hands in lap mudra

You can use this mudra (also known as the dhyani mudra) when you meditate. Rest your left hand on top of your right palm, with both palms facing up and the tips of the thumbs touching while resting on your lap. If you're a man, reverse this position, so your right hand is on top of your left palm. This hand gesture helps to create a state of enlightenment.

Lotus mudra

This mudra symbolises the opening of your heart and it's a good one to practise when you are feeling a bit down, lonely or needing support. With your hands centred in prayer, spread out your fingers, keeping the base of the palms, thumbs and little fingers connected. Spread the remaining fingers out and let them blossom outwards like the petals of a lotus flower opening up. Hold for 4 breaths, then close your hands, placing the fingernails of both hands on top of each other and bringing together the backs of the fingers.

Slowly roll your hands down further until the backs touch. Rest like this for a while before inhaling and moving your hands back into the prayer and flower opening positions. Do this several times if you find it helpful.

There are many other mudras, including hand, head, posture and internal lock gestures. So, once you have mastered these, do some research and learn about other ones.

Above: Dhyani mudra is a gesture of meditation that helps connect the body and mind energies and bring enlightenment.

Above: Lotus mudra relates to the opening of the heart and makes you feel supported and enlivened.

INTRODUCTION

GETTING STARTED

BALANCING & STANDING

FLOOR POSTURES

WORKOUTS MADE EASY

RELAXATION

Resources & acknowledgements

Further reading...

★ *A Life Worth Breathing* by Max Strom, Skyhorse Publishing, 2010

★ *Autobiography of a Yogi* by Paramahansa Yogananda, Self-Realization Fellowship, 2006

★ *Light on Life: The Journey to Wholeness, Inner Peace and Ultimate Freedom* by BKS Iyengar, Rodale 2008

★ *The Power of Now: A Guide to Spiritual Enlightenment* by Eckhardt Tolle, Hodder, 2001

Recommended websites...

★ www.zest.co.uk – expert health, fitness and beauty advice from the number one women's health magazine

★ www.yogamatters.com – yoga props, straps and blankets

Thanks...

With thanks to Yamarama (www.yamarama.com) and Sweaty Betty (www.sweatybetty.com) for supplying clothing.

Index